# The Family Therapy Workbook

**96** | Guided Interventions to Help Families Connect, Cope, and Heal

**Kathleen Mates-Youngman**, MFT, RYT200,
Best-Selling Author of *Couples Therapy Workbook*

Copyright © 2021 by Kathleen Mates-Youngman

Published by
PESI Publishing & Media
PESI, Inc
3839 White Ave
Eau Claire, WI 54703

Editing: Jenessa Jackson, PhD, and Lauren Hovde
Layout: Amy Rubenzer
Cover: Amy Rubenzer

ISBN: 9781683732990

Proudly printed in the United States

PESI
Publishing
& Media
pesipublishing.com

# Table of Contents

## part 1    Foundational Traits of Healthy Families

## part 2    Unique Family Challenges

# About the Author

**Kathleen Mates-Youngman** is a licensed marriage and family therapist and a registered yoga teacher in Orange County, California. She has been married to her high school sweetheart for thirty-five years, is the mother of three adult children, and is a Nana to two beautiful grandsons.

Kathleen considers time with family the most precious part of her life, yet—as with any family—there are periods of challenge. At these times, she makes it a priority to come from love and to practice compassion, healthy communication, validation, and respect in order to help the system find health once again. In this book, she shares her knowledge as a family member and a psychotherapist to help clinicians guide their clients to a similar place of health.

Kathleen specializes in couples therapy in her private practice, and she has trained other clinicians in couples therapy as a national speaker for PESI. Her first book, *Couples Therapy Workbook: 30 Guided Conversations to Re-Connect Relationships*, continues to be an Amazon bestseller, and she is excited to share her knowledge about working with families in her new book for clinicians.

# Introduction

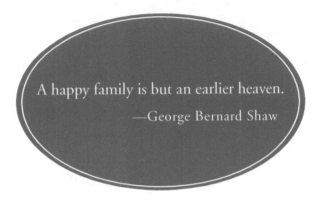

A happy family is but an earlier heaven.
—George Bernard Shaw

There are many definitions of *family*. According to the US Census Bureau, "A family is a group of two people or more related by birth, marriage, or adoption and residing together; all such people (including related subfamily members) are considered as members of one family."

As psychotherapists, when we are treating a family, we generally see one or both parents and children or stepchildren, and sometimes also extended family members and even pets. Whatever the configuration, though, there are always common goals. Family members want to feel close, loved, valued, respected, heard, safe, and tethered together, wherever they might be.

It's common for family members to worry that we may take one person's word over another's, with the kids often assuming that we will side with their parents, so we must let them know in the first session that "the client is the *family*." While we are not there to remain neutral, and may at times address one member more than another, we must reassure them that it is always our purpose to guide the whole system to greater health and happiness. We absolutely want them to feel assured that we are there to do what is in the best interest for each one of them and for the family as a whole.

It can be very challenging to be in the room with many different personalities, attitudes, temperaments, and emotional presentations. We are there in part to create a safe container, to reflect what we see and hear, and to make certain that each person feels seen, heard, and validated. We observe their verbal and nonverbal communication, and through our stance, words, tone, guidance, and interventions, we aim to create healthy shifts in the system while always offering unconditional positive regard.

Of course, we only have 50 minutes a week to accomplish our goals, so the work that continues at home is absolutely essential. As always, the clients need to work harder than the therapist, so sending them home with goals and assignments for the time between sessions is a great way to offer them the opportunity to reconnect and practice new skills. Doing so requires a great deal of vulnerability, so it's essential to emphasize the importance of being open and respectful as family members share with one another.

The purpose of *The Family Therapy Workbook* is to guide your clients to greater communication, understanding, health, and connection. The book addresses nine foundational traits of healthy families and nine unique family challenges, with home assignments for each topic. Each home assignment includes guidelines on how to have an informative conversation, as well as one or more experiential activities, which the family can process in subsequent sessions to address any questions or concerns and to solidify learning.

I have also included a "Therapist Preparation" section for each topic, which offers additional information that you may incorporate into your sessions. The preparation includes:

1. Psychoeducation
2. Impact of each topic on the family system
3. Long-term family goals
4. Therapist-assignment summaries
5. Therapist-client assignment wrap-up
6. Sample client conversation to introduce each topic

Not all families are experiencing the same degree of dysfunction, nor will they all be at the same developmental stage, so you must tailor each topic of discussion and assignment to your individual clients. Feel free to adjust the wording and assignment to fit the age and developmental stage of each family member, as well as the particular emotional challenges they are facing.

**When working on any of the unique family challenge topics, always assess family members for mental or physical health issues, and refer them to other professionals as necessary for medical or psychiatric assessments, support groups, and so on.**

By teaching your clients the foundational traits of a healthy family system, addressing their experience of practicing new skills at home, and processing the emotional impact of sharing as a family, you are guiding them to greater connection, openness, respect, and love. Finally, be sure to encourage your clients to enjoy this journey and to remember that they are all on the same team.

part 1

Foundational
Traits
of
Healthy
Families

# 1

# Healthy Communication

## Therapist Preparation

As a psychotherapist, you are likely to hear from families that they struggle with "communication." This struggle can result from many different factors that are or are not occurring in the family.

Some families simply do not communicate at all. They live somewhat parallel lives, intersecting only for school drop-off/pick-up, meals, and logistical interactions. Other families may communicate but mostly in a hierarchical manner that does not necessarily invite a back-and-forth flow of interaction between the power-holding adults and the power-yielding children. And still other families may communicate often, yet unfortunately they do so in a controlling, angry, punitive manner that discourages openness, vulnerability, and connection. Certainly, and fortunately, there are families that do communicate well, yet they, too, might still benefit from guided conversations and education that can strengthen an already healthy system.

## The Impact of Poor Communication on the Family System

1. There is a lack of communication or conversation between family members due to fear of conflict or stonewalling.
2. There are frequent arguments among some or all family members.
3. Communication is often misinterpreted due to cognitive distortions, assumptions, sender/receiver blocks, or interrupting.
4. There is a lack of understanding regarding triggers of conflict.
5. Family exhibits an unhealthy ratio of positive to negative interactions.

## Long-Term Family Goals

1. Family develops an open and respectful system that allows for communication and conflict without fear, stonewalling, or interruptions.
2. Family members express needs, opinions, and feelings without anger, defensiveness, or contempt.
3. Family understands and limits cognitive distortions and assumptions and uses tools and techniques to clarify communications.
4. Family understands and corrects the triggers for dysfunctional communication.
5. Family increases compliments, expressions of appreciation, and overall positive interactions.

On the following pages are three communication assignments to give to your clients one week at a time. In session, explain the topic to them using the sample conversation I have provided as a guide, and then describe the assignments to them, answering any questions they may have. If necessary, help the family modify the assignments to make them developmentally appropriate and understandable for all family members. Then send them home with the following assignments over the next three sessions, and process what they learned about family communication, as well as their experience of sharing about the topic with one another.

## Therapist Assignment Summaries

### Assignment #1: *Communication Conversation*

The purpose of this assignment is for the family to explore the true meaning of communication, as well as how it feels to communicate in *this* family. It is especially important that they understand the difference between hearing (perceiving sound) and listening (a conscious choice to receive and interpret words).

### Assignment #2: *Hello... Do You Hear Me?*

The purpose of this assignment is for each family member to practice being the "sender" by sharing a difficult experience and then having the "receiver" reflect what they just heard. It is important that the receiver does not simply recite what was said but reflect what they heard the sender say, as well as the feelings conveyed. "What I heard you say was... and you felt..."

### Assignment #3: *Communication Charades*

The purpose of this assignment is to understand the power and impact of nonverbal communication. Each family member will read a prompt and then act out an emotion without using words, while the others guess what it is.

Once your clients have completed all three healthy communication assignments, and you have processed each in session, review the following goals in order to solidify their new understanding of this important topic.

## Communication Assignments Wrap-Up

"Now that you have done all three of the healthy communication assignments, and we have talked about each in session, let's see what you have learned. Do you feel that you..."

1. Understand the true meaning of healthy communication in a family system?
   - More open and respectful interactions
   - Conflict is expressed without fear, intimidation, stonewalling, or interruptions
   - Sharing without anger, defensiveness, or contempt
   - Awareness of triggers for dysfunctional communication
   - Decrease in cognitive distortions
2. Understand the difference between hearing and listening?
   - Full attention, eye contact, nods
3. Understand how to reflect what was heard and correct it if necessary?
   - "What I hear you saying is..." "Correct me if I'm wrong..."

4. Understand the difference between verbal and nonverbal communication?
   - Body language, facial expressions, utterances (sighs, grunts, and so on)
5. Have increased positive interactions?
   - Compliments, sharing appreciation, smiles, hugs
6. A little closer and more connected as a family after spending three weeks working on healthy communication?
7. "On a scale of 1–10, with 1 being the worst and 10 the best, how well do you think your family communicates now?"

## Sample Conversation

*Communication* is defined many different ways, but generally speaking, it's the process of passing information from one person, the sender, to another person, the receiver. It's important to know that you communicate not only with words but also with your facial expressions, body language, and tone of voice.

When you are the "sender," healthy communication means that you feel safe to express your thoughts and that you feel truly listened to and understood when you do so. When you are the "receiver," healthy communication means that you don't just hear but that you also listen and are able to reflect what you heard, to be corrected if necessary, and to feel safe to respond respectfully. When you are just *hearing* someone, it's the same as merely hearing the noise around you but not really paying attention. When you are truly *listening*, you maintain eye contact, you might nod your head, you do not interrupt, and you don't think about what you are going to say next.

Another reason that communication can become challenging is due to what we call *cognitive distortions*. These are basically ways that our mind convinces us of something that is not accurate and, in turn, blocks our ability to achieve clear communication. Some examples are:

1. **Jumping to conclusions:** You think you know what another person is feeling or thinking.
2. **Personalization:** When someone is sharing something, you assume they are blaming or criticizing you.
3. **Blaming:** You assign responsibility for your feelings to someone else and attack them for it, as opposed to respectfully sharing a thought or complaint.
4. **Always being right:** You have to win an argument regardless of how it makes others feel.

As the member of a family, if you understand that you communicate both verbally and nonverbally, and that you are able to speak, listen, and respond with love and respect, you will all feel valued for who you are. You will also feel connected, close, and grateful to call one another your family.

# Questions to Explore with Family Members

1. On a scale of 1–10, with 1 being the worst and 10 being the best, how well do you think your family communicates?

   _____

   _____

2. Are there certain things that are more difficult to talk about than others?

   _____

   _____

3. Is there anything in particular that you think gets in the way of communication in your family?

   _____

   _____

4. Do the conversations ever get heated when you try to discuss important matters?

   _____

   _____

5. Would you like be able to talk more as a family and to each family member in a really healthy way?

   _____

   _____

I'm going to send you home today with one of three communication assignments that are going to benefit you in three ways:

1. First, you are going to practice a wonderful new ritual: a weekly family conversation date.

2. Next, you are going to learn about how each of you currently experiences communication in the family and how to create healthier family communication going forward.

3. And finally, by feeling listened to and respected, you are going to feel a greater sense of connection and emotional safety in the family.

*Always remember to be loving and respectful!*

# Communication Conversation

*The single biggest problem with communication*
*is the illusion that it has taken place.*
—George Bernard Shaw

Enjoy a nice conversation about communication in your family. Choose one person as the family secretary to take notes about the family responses. Then take turns asking the following questions. Go around the family one by one, answering each question according to how you feel. Remember always to be honest, kind, respectful, and loving.

1. What does communication mean to you?

_____

_____

_____

2. What is the difference between hearing and listening?

_____

_____

_____

3. Do you feel like you are really listened to when you are sharing things?

_____

_____

_____

4. Can you think of a time when you felt like you weren't understood?

_____

_____

_____

5. Are you ever scared to share things with your family?

_____

_____

_____

6. Do you feel like you are heard as much as everyone else in the family?

_____

_____

_____

7. Do you feel like we interrupt one another or let one another finish sentences?

_____

_____

_____

8. Do you feel like you (or we) engage in certain cognitive distortions?

_____

_____

_____

9. What do you think we could do to be better communicators?

_____

_____

_____

Share with one another how it felt to have this conversation. Have the family secretary bring the notes to your next therapy session, and let your therapist know what you learned about yourself and your family members.

# Hello . . . Do You Hear Me?

Just as we sometimes have fuzzy reception on our phones, we sometimes have fuzzy reception within our family. It's so important to be able to tell our story and to know that we were heard.

Have one family member read the following directions, and then begin the exercise:

- Think of a time when you were sad or mad. Now tell the family about it.

- Then pick someone in the family to tell you what they just heard you say, using these words: "What I hear you say is... and you felt..."

**Example:**

| | |
|---|---|
| Sender: | "The other day I was sad because I asked my friend to play with me and they said no." |
| Receiver: | "What I hear you say is that your friend didn't want to play with you the other day, and you felt really sad. I'm sorry you felt sad—I love you." |

Take turns doing this exercise, and then talk about how it felt to tell your story and feel heard.

# Communication Charades

Using words is not the only way you communicate. Your posture, facial expressions, tone of voice, and attitude all send messages as well.

Take turns silently reading each prompt, and then act it out without using words. The first person to guess the emotion you are feeling gets a high five.

1. You just won the lottery.

2. Your alarm didn't go off, and you are late for a flight.

3. You are watching a horror movie, and something really scary is about to happen.

4. Your best friend just moved far away.

5. You're watching a very dull show.

6. Someone you really don't like is talking to you.

7. Someone put your favorite outfit in the dryer and it shrank.

8. You have a fun day planned with all your favorite friends, foods, and activities.

9. You're cuddling your favorite pet or person.

Notice how much you were able to communicate without using words.

# 2

# Rituals, Traditions, and Fun

## Therapist Preparation

Rituals and traditions are key to creating family connection. They help cultivate a family identity, create a foundation of stability, and provide a sense of continuity. Rituals also offer the opportunity for fun and sharing, which can contribute to a lifetime of stories and memories.

Rituals can be as simple as setting a nice table for Sunday dinner, having a family movie night, or stopping for ice cream on the way home from school on the last day of every month. Traditions tend to have more history, often reaching back generations in a family. They create a sense of anticipation that brings everyone closer, and the days leading up to such traditions can be quite magical.

Families that engage in rituals and traditions tend to have a greater sense of shared meaning, deeper friendships, and the assurance that wherever they may go, they are always tethered to home.

## The Impact of a Lack of Rituals, Traditions, and Fun on the Family System

1. Family does not make special memories that create a family identity.
2. There is a lack of family structure, foundation, and connection.
3. Family members miss opportunities for sharing and bonding.
4. The home environment is more somber, and family members have a reduced desire to spend time at home
5. There is less opportunity for creativity, learning, and planned activities.

## Long-Term Family Goals

1. Family members learn about their family history and develop a family identity.
2. There are more opportunities for family time and connection.
3. Family has a greater sense of comfort and ease in the home.
4. Family understands the value of planning for fun, sharing experiences, gaining exposure to new surroundings and cultures, and learning new skills.

On the following pages are three assignments pertaining to rituals, traditions, and fun, which you can give to your clients one week at a time. In session, explain the topic to them using the sample conversation I have provided as a guide, and then describe the assignments to them, answering any questions they may have. If necessary, help the family modify the assignments to make them developmentally appropriate and understandable for all family members. Then send them home with the following assignments over the next three sessions, and process what they learned about rituals, traditions, and fun, as well as their experience of sharing about the topic with one another, in each subsequent session.

## Therapist Assignment Summaries

**Assignment #1:** *Rituals, Traditions, and Fun Conversation*

The purpose of this assignment is for the family to explore the importance of incorporating rituals, celebrating traditions, and having fun. This conversation allows each family member to share their own special feelings and memories, and it suggests more ideas for activities that the family can enjoy together.

**Assignment #2:** *Family Fun Day*

The purpose of this assignment is for each family member to create five ideas for family fun. This activity emphasizes the importance of rituals, traditions, and fun in developing a family identity, as well as in creating healthy balance in life. Once again, it also allows each family member to participate and be heard.

**Assignment #3:** *Family Collage*

The purpose of this assignment is to creatively explore how each family member sees and experiences the family, as well as what they would like to see in the family going forward. It also offers an opportunity for humor, sensitivity, and sharing in a nonjudgmental, unconditional manner.

Once they have completed all the rituals, traditions, and fun assignments, review the following goals to solidify their new understanding of this important topic.

## Rituals, Traditions, and Fun Assignment Wrap-Up

"Now that you have done three rituals, traditions, and fun assignments, and we have talked about each in session, let's see what you have learned. Do you feel that you..."

1. Understand the importance of rituals, traditions, and fun for the family?
2. Know what the favorite and most memorable rituals and traditions are for each family member?
3. Are able to create new rituals, traditions, and opportunities for fun?
4. Are going to practice having fun as a family?
5. See how rituals, traditions, and fun are important to your family now?
6. Are a little closer and more connected as a family after spending three weeks working on rituals, traditions, and fun?

## Sample Conversation

Rituals and traditions are similar, yet they have some very subtle differences. *Rituals* are often special things we say or do to honor special moments or transitions in life. For instance, a wedding celebration, a graduation ceremony, and even a memorial service are rituals that mark the importance of each event and allow us to remember these special times forever. They can also be special things we often do to feel connected and loved, like having a more formal Sunday dinner or sharing the favorite part of our day as we settle in to sleep at night.

*Traditions* are very similar, yet they often incorporate activities that have been handed down through the generations. For instance, traditions might include decorating the house with family heirlooms during the holidays, cooking from generational family recipes at special times of the year, or returning to a favorite vacation spot year after year.

And of course we all know what *fun* is, yet we don't always give ourselves permission to make it a priority in our family and life. Having fun together allows us to let go of daily responsibilities and worries, to see one another through a different lens, and to be a little silly.

The more you combine rituals, traditions and fun into your family life, the more you will feel like you belong, are all on the same team, and have one another's backs. These activities will also give you something to look forward to, provide you with things to do together, and allow you to create wonderful memories you can share for years to come.

# Questions to Explore with Family Members

1. What do you most like doing together as a family?

   _____

   _____

2. Is there something you do every week that you look forward to?

   _____

   _____

3. What team name would you give your family?

   _____

   _____

4. Who usually makes the plans in your family?

   _____

   _____

5. What is your favorite holiday to celebrate with your family?

   _____

   _____

I'm going to send you home today with one of three rituals, traditions, and fun assignments that are going to benefit you in three ways:

1. First, you are going to practice a wonderful new ritual: a weekly family conversation date.

2. Next, you are going to discover what rituals and traditions mean to each of you and create new ones for your family.

3. And finally, you are going to have fun together, be creative, and learn how each of you sees the family now and in the future.

*Always remember to be loving and respectful!*

# Rituals, Traditions, and Fun Conversation

*When in doubt, choose the kids. There will be plenty of time later to choose work.*
—Anna Quindlen

Enjoy a nice conversation about rituals, traditions, and fun in your family. Have one person ask the following questions, or take turns doing so. Choose one person as the family secretary to take notes about the family responses. Go around the family one by one, answering each question according to how you feel. Remember always to be honest, kind, respectful, and loving.

1.  What do rituals and traditions mean to you?

_____

_____

_____

2.  Do we have any weekly rituals that you really enjoy?

_____

_____

_____

3.  What is your favorite time of year and why?

_____

_____

_____

4. What are your favorite family traditions?

_____

_____

_____

5. When did you last have fun with our family?

_____

_____

_____

6. Do you have any ideas for more family rituals, traditions, or fun?

_____

_____

_____

# Family Fun Day

Gather a cardboard box about the size of a shoebox to use as a family fun suggestion box. Decorate it together with words, pictures, and anything else that represents your family.

Have each family member write five ideas for fun family activities on separate pieces of paper and put them in the box.

Shake the box, and take turns choosing one activity a week for your family to enjoy.

After the activity, share what you enjoyed most about spending time together.

# Family Collage

**Materials:**

- Large piece of poster board for each family member

- Magazines

- Scissors

- Glue

Tear or cut out pictures from various magazines that represent your family to you. Use any pictures that make you think of the personalities, memories, feelings, and things you see or would like to see in your family. Glue the pictures on to the poster board in any arrangement.

When you are done, take turns showing your collage to your family and share what it means to you.

Have a conversation about the things you learned about one another from seeing each person's collage.

# 3

# Respecting One Another

## Therapist Preparation

We encourage the family members we work with to treat one another with respect, yet we shouldn't assume that they truly understand what this means in the context of the family. The goal is to convey to families that *respect* is a way of treating or thinking about someone that shows you appreciate, admire, and hold them in high regard.

And how do we show other people that we respect them? There are many ways, but generally we are thoughtful, attentive, polite, and courteous. We truly listen, let them finish their sentences, encourage them, say "please" and "thank you," and manage our anger without becoming insulting, threatening, or physical.

It's also necessary for families to learn how to show respect for their possessions and the world around them. This might include walking on the sidewalk instead of cutting across the grass, putting toys away, hanging up clothes, watering a plant before it begins to wilt, or being quiet in a library or church.

Teaching families that we also communicate our thoughts nonverbally is very important. An internal critical thought might result in a roll of the eyes, whereas a kind inner thought might result in a smile or a soft touch. And of course, parents must understand that they set the bar and model the behaviors that their children then consciously or unconsciously replicate.

## The Impact of a Lack of Respect on the Family System

1. There is a lack of polite interactions among family members.
2. Appropriate boundaries are lacking between family members.
3. Family members disregard rules and expectations.
4. Family members experience injuries to self-esteem and feel devalued and unappreciated.
5. Family is characterized by disconnection, discouragement, and depression.

## Long-Term Family Goals

1. Family members exhibit improvements in open, polite, and courteous conversations.
2. Parents clearly communicate boundaries, rules, and expectations, and children will adhere to these guidelines.
3. Family increases the amount of positive interactions and communications they have with one another.

4. Family members prioritize family time.

5. Family more effectively works together to care for their home and possessions.

On the following pages are three family respect assignments to give to your clients one week at a time. In session, explain the topic to them using the sample conversation I have provided as a guide, and then describe the assignments to them, answering any questions they might have. If necessary, help the family modify the assignments to make them developmentally appropriate and understandable for all family members. Then send them home with the following assignments over the next three sessions, and process what they learned about respect in the family, as well as their experience of sharing about the topic with one another, in each subsequent session.

## Therapist Assignment Summaries

**Assignment #1:** *A Conversation about Respect*

The purpose of this assignment is for the family to explore the true meaning of respect, as well as how they show and experience respect in the family. It is especially important that they understand why respect is so important and that respect extends to people, possessions, situations, and the environment.

**Assignment #2:** *Practicing Respect*

The purpose of this assignment is for each family member to practice showing respect through their words and actions. When a family member does something respectful, it's important that other members reflect what they noticed so it reinforces this positive trait for the whole family. For instance, "I noticed you picking up after yourself, and I really appreciate that. Thank you."

**Assignment #3:** *Chatting Respectfully about Respect*

The purpose of this assignment is to reinforce what family members have learned throughout the week about speaking and behaving respectfully. Each family member has the opportunity to learn from one another and to feel unified as a caring and kind family.

Once they have completed all three family respect assignments, review the following goals to solidify their new understanding of this significant topic.

## Family Respect Assignments Wrap-Up

"Now that you have done all three family respect assignments, and we have talked about each in session, let's see what you have learned. Do you feel that you…"

1. Understand the true meaning of respect in a family system?

2. Understand the difference between speaking and behaving respectfully?

3. Had more positive interactions when you treated one another, your possessions, and the environment with respect?

4. Noticed the positive impact on your relationships when you are being treated with respect?

5. Are a little closer and more connected as a family after spending three weeks working on respect?

## Sample Conversation

*Respect* is defined many different ways, but generally speaking, it is a way of showing through your words and actions that you appreciate, admire, and hold one another in high regard. You do this by being thoughtful, attentive, polite, and courteous. Examples include letting other people finish their sentences, truly listening, being encouraging, saying "please" and "thank you," and managing your anger without becoming insulting, threatening, or physical. You also communicate respect through your actions. If you are listening to someone and you roll your eyes, they are going to feel disrespected, but if you instead smile and nod your head, they will feel that you are listening and interested, and will therefore feel respected.

It's also important to treat your possessions with respect. Doing things like hanging up your clothes, putting your toys away, watering the plants, being gentle with your bikes, and keeping your car clean show that you care about your possessions and appreciate having them. You can also be respectful to the environment by throwing away trash, recycling, walking on the sidewalk instead of across the grass, not wasting water, and even by being quiet when you are in a library or church.

As family members, if you practice showing respect through your words and actions, you will each feel that you are respected for who you are and that you all greatly value your relationships, your possessions, and the world around you.

# Questions to Explore with Family Members

1. On a scale of 1–10, with 1 being the worst and 10 being the best, how respectful do you think you are as a family?

   _____

   _____

2. Do you think that you speak to one another politely?

   _____

   _____

3. Are you each respectful of the rules and consequences in your family?

   _____

   _____

4. Children, do you understand that your parents are in charge of the family and want what is best for everyone?

   _____

   _____

5. Do you think it's important to take care of your home and your things?

   _____

   _____

I'm going to send you home today with one of three family respect assignments that will benefit you in three ways:

1. First, you are going to practice a wonderful new ritual: a weekly family conversation date.

2. Next, you are going to learn about how you each currently experience respect in the family and how to create healthier family respect going forward.

3. And finally, by feeling and showing respect, you are going to appreciate one another, your possessions, and the world around you much more, and you will feel proud to be a member of this great family.

*Always remember to be loving and respectful!*

# Respect Conversation

*A person's a person, no matter how small.*
—Dr. Seuss

Enjoy a nice conversation about the importance of respect in your family. Choose one person as the family secretary to take notes about the family responses. Then take turns asking the following questions. Go around the family one by one, answering each question according to how you feel. Remember always to be honest, kind, respectful, and loving.

1. How do you define respect?

_____

_____

2. What makes you feel respected?

_____

_____

3. Do you think it's important to treat one another with respect? Why?

_____

_____

4. Do you feel that it's okay to be your unique self in this family?

_____

_____

5. Do you see why it's important to treat our home, possessions, animals, and plants with respect?

_____

_____

6. Is there anything else that we can do as a family to show one another more respect?

_____

_____

# Practicing Respect

Over the next week, say the following words to one another as often as you can:

1. Please.

2. Thank you.

3. I love you.

4. Can I help you with anything?

5. Good morning.

6. Good night.

7. Have a nice day.

8. How was your day?

And...

Over the next week, do the following things as often as you can:

1. Hug one another.

2. Smile at one another.

3. Pay one another a compliment.

4. Make your bed.

5. Do a chore that you haven't been asked to do.

Put these lists in a place where each family member will see them every day. Feel free to add anything to these lists that might benefit your family. Check the lists every day to remind yourself of the goals for the week.

# Chatting Respectfully About Respect

At the end of the week, carve out some time to talk about your experience with the lists in the previous assignment. Ask the following questions:

1. How easy or difficult was it to do and say these things during the week?

_____

_____

2. Which words or actions were easiest for you? Which were difficult?

_____

_____

3. How did it make you feel to experience these words and actions from our family members?

_____

_____

4. Do you think we should continue to practice these respectful words and behaviors?

_____

_____

5. Are there any words or behaviors that you would like to add to the list?

_____

_____

6. Is there anything we can do to make it easier to act respectfully as a family?

_____

_____

# 4

# Expressing Anger and Managing Conflict

## Therapist Preparation

Although anger is a basic emotion that serves an adaptive and protective purpose, it is often an emotion that families struggle with. Some families do not tolerate this emotion at all. In other families, only the parents are allowed to express anger. And in many families, anger is expressed openly but in a manner that injures feelings, friendship, and connection.

As clinicians, it's our job to help clients explore and express any feelings of anger, to guide them toward an understanding of what underlies the anger, and finally, to empower them to share their anger in a caring, respectful, and productive manner. This means that we educate family members about how they can express their anger without blaming, devaluing, or becoming aggressive. We help them express how and why they feel as they do, and we teach them how to hear others do the same without becoming defensive or stonewalling. We also guide them toward repair and growth after conflict.

## The Impact of Inappropriate Anger on the Family System

1. Family is characterized by defensiveness and blame.
2. Family members do not take responsibility for their own actions.
3. There is aggressive behavior in one or all members.
4. Family interactions are often characterized by disagreements and stonewalling.
5. Family members exhibit passive-aggressive behavior.
6. Family members may shut down and avoid interacting with one another.
7. Family is characterized by sadness, discouragement, and lack of repair.

## Long-Term Family Goals

1. Family reduces expressions of anger and increases healthy expressions of feelings.
2. Family members become aware of their feelings and triggers, and they will develop the ability to self-soothe, contain, and communicate in a productive manner.
3. Family improves their ability to communicate in an empathic, compassionate, and validating manner.
4. Family members learn mindfulness skills to become aware of their feelings as they arise.
5. Family creates a safe environment in which they can express their complaints, concerns, hurt, frustration, and general needs.
6. Family improves their ability to turn toward one another, accept influence, and repair conflicts.

On the following pages you'll find three expression of anger assignments to give to your clients one week at a time. In session, explain the topic to them using the sample conversation I have provided as a guide, and then describe the assignments to them, answering any questions they may have. If necessary, help the family modify the assignments to make them developmentally appropriate and understandable for all family members. Then send them home with the following assignments over the next three sessions, and process what they learned about communicating anger, as well as their experience of sharing about the topic with one another, in each subsequent session.

## Therapist Assignment Summaries

**Assignment #1:** *Expressing Anger Conversation*

The purpose of this assignment is for the family to explore how each member feels about anger in the family. Do they understand what angers them and why? Are they allowed to express anger, do they feel heard, and is there ultimately repair?

**Assignment #2:** *Where Is My Anger and What Is It Telling Me?*

The purpose of this assignment is to have clients begin to notice where they feel anger in their body when they become triggered. They will then have a chance to explore what the angry thoughts are and what sad or fearful thoughts they might have beneath the anger.

**Assignment #3:** *Mindfulness to Minimize Anger*

The purpose of this three-part exercise is to teach clients mindfulness skills to help them become aware of feelings as they experience them and to self-soothe, contain, and ask for what they need.

Once your clients have completed all three of the expressing anger and managing conflict assignments, and you have processed each in session, review the following goals to solidify their new understanding of this important topic.

## Expression of Anger Assignments Wrap-Up

"Now that you have done all three expression of anger assignments, and we have talked about each in session, let's see what you have learned. Do you feel that you…"

1. Are more aware of your feelings of anger when they come up?
2. Are more aware of what triggers your anger and the feelings of sadness or fear that may occur with it?
3. Have more tools to self-soothe when you are feeling upset?
4. As a family are able to talk about angry feelings in a respectful way instead of becoming contemptuous and hurtful?
5. Are able to really listen to one another's complaints and repair any hurt feelings that come from conflicts?
6. Are able to handle anger as a family now?
7. Are closer and more connected as a family after spending three weeks working on expressing anger in a healthy way?

## Sample Conversation

We are going to be exploring anger over the next few weeks, and I know this topic can be very difficult for a lot of people. We often think of anger as being a bad emotion, but it's actually one of the six basic emotions, which also include happiness, sadness, fear, surprise, and disgust. We are all hardwired with these emotions because they helped primitive humans to survive.

Many things can cause you to feel angry, and it's important to pay attention to what the causes are. For example, are you feeling powerless? Do you feel like you're in danger? Are your values or beliefs at risk? These sorts of experiences can understandably result in anger, and it's important to address the situation when you are having those feelings.

For example:

- "I'm feeling powerless right now, and what I need is to have some control over this situation and have my needs heard."

- "I'm feeling a little unsafe right now, and what I need is to talk calmly about this."

- "I'm feeling like my values and beliefs don't matter to you, and I really need to have them respected."

Unfortunately, when we don't manage our anger with clear communication, we can do a lot of harm to our relationships. And when we aren't interested in understanding why someone is angry, we also harm our relationships. So we want to practice expressing our anger in a way that allows us to be heard and respected, and we want to hear when someone else is angry with us so we can find out why and do what we can to repair the situation.

# Questions to Explore with Family Members

1. On a scale of 1-10, with 1 being the least angry and 10 being the most, how angry can things get in your family?

   _____

   _____

2. Is it acceptable in your family to share a complaint or talk about something that has made you angry?

   _____

   _____

3. Do any of you get angry so fast that you don't even notice when it happens?

   _____

   _____

4. Do you know that sometimes when you get angry you are actually really sad or scared underneath the anger?

   _____

   _____

5. When you do get angry at one another, are you able to make up after?

   _____

   _____

6. Would you like to be able to express anger in a healthy way as a family?

   _____

   _____

I'm going to send you home today with one of three expression of anger assignments that are going to benefit you in three ways:

1. First, you are going to have a conversation about expressing anger in a healthy way for your family conversation date.

2. Next, you are going to learn to be aware of where you feel anger in your body and what thoughts and feelings of sadness and fear lie beneath the angry surface.

3. And finally, you will learn mindfulness techniques to help you self-soothe when you are angry, contain your anger so you can share your feelings and ask for what you need, and work together to repair any hurt feelings.

*Always remember to be loving and respectful!*

# Expressing Anger Conversation

*Where there is anger, there is always pain underneath.*
—Eckhart Tolle

Enjoy a nice conversation about the importance of expressing anger and managing conflict in a healthy way in your family. Choose one person as the family secretary to take notes about the family responses. Then take turns asking the following questions. Go around the family one by one, answering each question according to how you feel. Remember to always be honest, kind, respectful, and loving.

1.  Do you feel like it's okay to be angry sometimes?

_____

_____

_____

2.  Do you ever get scared when any of us is angry or arguing?

_____

_____

_____

3.  How do you feel when one of us is angry with you?

_____

_____

_____

4. When you've been angry, even if you have been punished, has someone comforted you after?

_____

_____

_____

5. What makes you most angry here in the family or in life in general?

_____

_____

_____

6. What helps you to calm down when you are angry?

_____

_____

_____

7. Is there anything else we can do as a family to express anger or resolve conflicts in a healthy way?

_____

_____

_____

# Where Is My Anger and What Is It Telling Me?

1. Draw a stick figure of a body in the space below. Then close your eyes and think about the last time you were angry. What had just happened? What made you most angry about it?

Notice how you are feeling in your body right now. Where are you feeling your anger? Your tension? Any sadness? Any fear? Now open your eyes and draw on your stick figure where you felt any of these feelings. Use colors and marks that represent your feelings.

2. For this next activity write words or sentences above the line that express why you were angry. Next, write words or sentences below the line that express any sad or fearful thoughts you were also having. And finally, share this with your family. Remember to be caring and respectful with one another.

## ANGER

Example: "I was angry that my friend wouldn't play with me."

_____

_____

_____

_____

_____

_____

## FEELINGS UNDER MY ANGER

Example: "I was scared that my friend didn't like me anymore."

_____

_____

_____

_____

_____

# Mindfulness to Minimize Anger
## Letting Go of Tension Exercise

Have one family member read the instructions below, and then do the exercise together as a family.

- Close your eyes, and take a few deep breaths in through your nose and out through your mouth.

- Gradually tense your entire body, beginning with your facial muscles and then moving to your shoulders, gut, thighs, calves, and feet. Hold for a count of 10.

- Then relax your muscles, starting from your face down to your toes.

- Notice how your body feels when you let go of tension.

- Feel the tingling sensation throughout your body.

- Notice your breathing slowing down.

Now open your eyes and share how your body and mind feel after this exercise.

_____

_____

_____

_____

_____

_____

_____

As a family, practice this exercise every day this week to teach yourselves this valuable tool for releasing tension when you are angry.

# Mindfulness to Minimize Anger
## Breathing through Anger

Have one family member read the instructions below, and then do the exercises together as a family.

- Sit comfortably in a chair.

- Close your eyes.

- Take a few minutes to let your body settle down.

- Then take a breath in through your nose, slowly counting to four... 1... 2... 3... 4... and then exhaling slowly to a count of four... 1... 2... 3... 4.

- Repeat five times.

Now open your eyes and share how your body and mind feel after this exercise.

_____

_____

_____

_____

_____

_____

_____

_____

_____

As a family, practice this exercise every day this week to teach yourself this valuable tool for self-soothing when you are angry.

# Mindfulness to Minimize Anger
## Sensory Exercise for Anger

Have one family member read the instructions below, and then do the exercise together as a family.

- Stand inside or outside your home, apart from one another.

- Close your eyes.

- Take a few breaths, inhaling and exhaling slowly through your nose.

- Now open your eyes and notice what you see around you.

- Notice the colors and shapes in your environment.

- Next, notice any scents around you.

- Now walk around and touch some objects around you.

- Notice the textures—rough, smooth—and how they feel—cold, warm.

- Now notice any sounds or silence around you.

- Once again close your eyes.

- Take a few more slow breaths through your nose.

Now open your eyes slowly and take a moment to notice how your body and mind feel after this exercise.

As a family, practice this exercise every day this week to teach yourselves this valuable tool for self-soothing and containing your feelings when you are angry.

# 5

# Family Values

## Therapist Preparation

Every family has its own unique culture, which is generally driven by its value system. Family values are often passed down from generation to generation, and they give the family a sense of community and closeness, resulting in a set of beliefs and ideals that guide them socially, emotionally, morally, and behaviorally.

You can view family values as following a hierarchical structure, beginning with foundational beliefs and priorities, proceeding to emotional needs and care, moving next to behavioral actions and boundaries, and finally, ending with moral and ethical actions inside and outside the home. As psychotherapists, it's important to raise the topic of values with families and to help guide them in implementing and nurturing the values they hold dear.

When introducing values to families, it can be helpful to identify categories of values so they can then list things within each category that they do, or would like to do, to strengthen the presence of these values in their family. Some examples of values may be; time spent together, outdoor activities, time with friends, enjoying meals together, vacations, caring for the home, community service, nurturing physical and emotional health, or religion and spirituality.

## The Impact of Unclear Values on the Family System

1. Family members exhibit a lack of care for the family home and their belongings.
2. There is tension around chores, responsibilities, and assisting others.
3. Family members are disrespectful of one another's feelings, points of view, and needs.
4. Family members lack empathy, are disinterested in one another's lives, and have no desire for togetherness.
5. There are few family activities, dinners, or vacations.
6. Family is not involved in community care, volunteer activities, or outreach of any kind.

## Long-Term Family Goals

1. Family expresses and models how to care for and appreciate their home and belongings.
2. Family members work as a team and take personal responsibility.
3. Family is patient, honest, polite, caring, and open-minded with one another.
4. Family shows compassion and respect and engages in conflict without contempt or violence.

5. Family participates in a greater number of family activities and conversations that facilitate connection, learning, and growth for all.

6. Family members model what it means to maintain a healthy work ethic, take pride in one's accomplishments, be financially responsible, and show respect for others.

7. Family adds value to the community and world.

On the following pages are three family values assignments to give to your clients one week at a time. In session, explain the topic to them using the sample conversation I have provided as a guide, and then describe the assignments to them, answering any questions they may have. If necessary, help the family modify the assignments to make them developmentally appropriate and understandable for all family members. Then send them home with the following assignments over the next three sessions, and process what they learned about their family values, as well as their experience of sharing about the topic with one another, in each subsequent session.

## Therapist Assignment Summaries

**Assignment #1:** *Family Values Conversation*

The purpose of this assignment is for the family to explore the true meaning of "values," as well as their own family value system. Each family member will then explore their own individual values.

**Assignment #2:** *Family Values List*

The purpose of this assignment is to create a family values list. Each family member will share an answer in each of the given categories.

**Assignment #3:** *Family Mission Statement*

The purpose of this assignment is to create a family mission statement and motto based on the family values they identified in the previous assignment.

Once your clients have completed all three of the family values assignments, and you have processed each in session, review the following goals to solidify their new understanding of this crucial topic.

## Family Values Assignment Wrap-Up

Now that you have done all three of the family values assignments, and we have talked about them in session, let's see what you have learned. Do you feel that you..."

1. Understand the true meaning of a value?

2. Know what your family values are?

3. Are able to help nurture these values for the family?

4. Are committed to practicing healthy family values?

5. Are a little closer and more connected as a family after spending three weeks working on family values?

## Sample Conversation

We are going to be talking about your family values over the next several weeks. Values are the ideals that are most important to you, so you need to know what they are and whether you are living in line with those values. When you are living in accordance with your values, you feel better about yourself.

And when you are practicing those values in the family, you feel more loved, connected, and fulfilled as a group.

Every family has its own unique culture, which is really a result of that family's particular values. Some values are passed down from generation to generation, and they give your family a sense of being a team. Other values you develop and practice together, and they can shift over time depending on your family's progress. For instance, when your children are young, you may really value reading books and singing songs at bedtime, and when they are older, you may not do that, but you may be spend time talking about school, friendships, and other concerns. Healthy families are intentional about knowing and practicing family values, so this is a really significant topic for you to explore.

There are also many different categories or types of values. It helps to think of them as a pyramid:

- The foundation is the things you do to create a healthy family system, such as creating a caring, safe, and respectful home environment; modeling beliefs, priorities, and healthy communication; and tending to emotional needs.
- Next is the way you treat your home, your belongings, your finances, and your activities, as well as how you maintain healthy boundaries.
- Then comes how you teach and model social values and morals, including work ethic, educational outlook, and political beliefs.
- This is followed by how you care for the community, country, planet, and so on.
- Finally, at the top of the pyramid are your beliefs about topics such as spirituality, meaning, purpose, and life goals.

It's so important to know what you really value and to take actions that incorporate your values into your everyday life. Values are like a compass in that that they help you move in the right direction, make good decisions, set priorities, and reset your course if necessary.

# Questions to Explore with
# Family Members

1. On a scale of 1–10, with 1 being the worst and 10 being the best, how clear are you on what your family values really are?

   _____

   _____

2. Do you think it's necessary to respect one another's values?

   _____

   _____

3. Does it make sense to you that you may not all have the same values?

   _____

   _____

4. Do you think it's important to live by your values and not be swayed by what others think?

   _____

   _____

5. Would you like to work as a family to have a really solid foundation of healthy values?

   _____

   _____

I'm going to send you home today with one of three family values assignments that are going to benefit you in three ways:

1. First, you are going to have a nice family conversation date to talk about your family values.

2. Next, you are going to learn what each of you values and how you define that. From those lists, you are going to create a family mission statement and a family motto.

3. And finally, by exploring your values and your family's values, you are going to strengthen your sense of connection and of being on the same team.

*Always remember to be loving and respectful!*

# Family Values Conversation

*Tell me what you pay attention to and I will tell you who you are.*
—José Ortega y Gasset

Enjoy a nice conversation about the importance of having family values and living in accordance with these values. Choose one person as the family secretary to take notes about the family responses. Then take turns asking the following questions. Go around the family one by one, answering each question according to how you feel. Remember to always be honest, kind, respectful, and loving.

1. What would you say are the most important things to you in your life?

_____

_____

_____

2. Is there anything you feel you couldn't live without?

_____

_____

_____

3. Do you think it's important to take care of your possessions? Why or why not?

_____

_____

_____

4. Do you think it's important to be nice to one another? Why or why not?

_____

_____

_____

5. What do you think our family cares about the most?

_____

_____

_____

6. What makes you the proudest of our family?

_____

_____

_____

7. When do you have the most fun with our family?

_____

_____

_____

8. Is there anything else you think we could do to practice our family values?

_____

_____

_____

# Family Values Chart

**Materials:**

- Large piece of poster board

- Large marker

Begin by having each family member answer the following questions, and have the family secretary write the answers down. You can either use a separate piece of paper or the table provided on the next page for this activity.

1. What do we do to nurture our **family values**? (e.g., communicate respectfully, care for our property, show interest)

2. What **social values** are important to us? (e.g., peace, freedom, honesty, community care, respect, volunteering)

3. What **work/education values** are important to us? (e.g., working as a team, giving our best effort, studying)

4. What **moral values** are important to us? (e.g., trustworthiness, persistence, patience, personal responsibility)

5. What **recreational values** are important to us? (e.g., family movie/game nights, vacations, traditions, sportsmanship)

6. What **religious/spiritual values** are important to us? (e.g., compassion, nonviolence, treating others as we would like to be treated, prayer)

7. Regardless of party, what **political values** are important to us? (e.g., democracy, patriotism, liberty, justice, equality)

8. What **economic values** are important to us? (e.g., saving, having an allowance, spending, earning)

**Feel free to add any more categories that are important to you.**

# Family Values Chart

| Family | Social | Work/Education | Moral | Recreational | Religious/Spiritual | Political | Economic | Other |
|--------|--------|----------------|-------|--------------|---------------------|-----------|----------|-------|
|        |        |                |       |              |                     |           |          |       |

# Our Family Mission Statement and Motto

Using the words you added to each family values category in the previous assignment, create your own family mission statement and motto. You can use the following template and modify it however you would like.

We are the _____ family.
                     (last name)

Our core foundational values are:

_____

_____

We show our commitment to these values by:

_____

_____

We show our respect for our community by:

_____

_____

We show our friends that we value them by:

_____

_____

We show our teachers and mentors that we value them by:

_____

_____

Our hopes and dreams for our family are:

_____

_____

We are helping to create these hopes and dreams by:

_____

_____

Our hopes and dreams for the planet are:

_____

_____

We are helping to create these hopes and dreams by:

_____

_____

The things that bring us a sense of meaning and purpose are:

_____

_____

Having a clear sense of our family values has made us feel:

_____

_____

And finally, given all that we have just learned about our family values, our family motto is:

_____

_____

# 6

# Parenting Styles and Temperament

## Therapist Preparation

From the moment a family first enters our therapy room, we begin gathering information about the dynamics of the system. We take note of where they sit, the expressions on their faces, the positioning of their bodies, and the ease or difficulty with which each individual opens up.

We also want to observe the particular parenting styles and the temperament of each family member. Parenting style has a tremendous impact on behavior, as does the temperament of each person in the family system.

## Parenting Styles

In the 1960s, developmental psychologist Diane Baumrind, PhD, identified four parenting styles: authoritarian, permissive, neglectful, and authoritative. Her research found that parenting style impacts discipline style, communication style, nurturance, expectations, and children's behavior. Therefore, understanding our clients parenting style is key information as we develop a treatment plan for the family.

1. **Authoritarian/Disciplinarian**
   - Strict, inflexible disciplinarians with little negotiation
   - Punishment common
   - Rules unexplained
   - One-way communication between parent and child
   - Typically less nurturing
   - High expectations

2. **Permissive/Indulgent**
   - Limited or no rules
   - Children left to figure things out
   - Open communication but little direction
   - Generally warm and nurturing
   - Minimal expectations

3. **Neglectful/Uninvolved**
   - No particular discipline style
   - Limited communication
   - Little nurturing
   - Few expectations

4. **Authoritative**
- Rules of discipline are clear and reasons are explained
- Frequent age-appropriate communication
- Nurturing
- Expectations and goals are high, yet reasonable and clear
- Input from children is allowed

## Four Temperament Traits

Temperament refers to biologically based traits that impact how we react to our world, behave, and interact with others. Though these innate traits are not learned, they can be influenced by family dynamics and culture. Learning about a child's temperament can help parents understand their behavior, and have appropriate expectations. When parents understand how a child's temperament is similar to or different from their own, they are more able to build on their strengths, and meet their individual needs.

As a note, there is often overlap between these categories.

1. Sanguine: These children are enthusiastic, active, social, talkative, charismatic, extroverted, outgoing, and risk-seeking.
2. Choleric: These children are short-tempered, fast, irritable, extroverted, independent, decisive, goal-oriented, and ambitious. They also tend to be natural leaders.
3. Melancholic: These children are analytical, wise, quiet, detail-oriented, introverted, self-reliant, reserved, thoughtful, often anxious, and perfectionistic. They tend to be deep thinkers and feelers.
4. Phlegmatic: These children are relaxed, peaceful, quiet, easygoing, sympathetic, caring, accommodating, and reserved.

In young children, temperaments are also often described as easy, difficult, or slow to warm up. An "easy child" is generally in a positive mood, prone to regular routines, easily adaptable to new experiences or people, moderately expressive when happy or sad, and moderate in activity level. A "difficult child" generally reacts negatively, is highly active, cries frequently, tends to have irregular routines, adapts slowly to new experiences or people, and is very expressive when happy or sad. Finally, a "slow-to-warm-up child" is generally low in activity level, somewhat negative, not very adaptable to new people and situations, and less expressive when happy or sad.

## Nine Dimensions of Temperament

In 1965, Doctors Chess, Thomas, and Birch, also identified nine dimensions of temperament that they broke into different ages. The following table describes the nine dimensions as they appear in children and adults. Learning about these dimensions may help parents understand how temperament impacts their life and relationship with their child.

| Nine Dimensions of Temperament | | |
|---|---|---|
| | **Child** | **Adult** |
| **Activity Level** | | |
| High | Squirmy and active | Difficulty sitting still, active |
| Low | Likes quiet and stillness | Prefers sedentary |
| **Distractibility** | | |
| High | Sensitive to discomfort | Difficulty concentrating |
| Low | Not easily bothered | Pays attention appropriately |
| **Adaptability** | | |
| High | Quickly adapts to new situations | Transitions easily |
| Low | Cries or stays close to parent | Needs time to transition prior to approaching |
| **Intensity** | | |
| High | Strong positive or negative reactions | |
| Low | Muted emotional reactions | |
| **Regularity** | | |
| High | Predictable appetite, sleep, elimination schedule | |
| Low | Unpredictable appetite, sleep, elimination schedule | |
| **Approachability** | | |
| High | Excitedly approaches new people or situations | |
| Low | Hesitant to approach | |
| **Sensitivity** | | |
| High | Sensitive to sounds, taste, touch, temperature, new foods, or strange environments | |
| Low | Not bothered by sensory or physical stimuli, open to new foods, experiences, or environments | |
| **Persistence** | | |
| High | Pushes through obstacles, not easily frustrated | |
| Low | Easily frustrated, gives up when met with obstacles | |
| **Mood** | | |
| Positive | Cheerful and positive about life | |
| Negative | Serious, observant | |

## The Impact of Each Parenting Style on the Family System

1. Authoritarian parenting often results in children who are obedient, but these children are less happy, less socially confident, and lack healthy self-esteem.

2. Permissive parenting often results in children who have difficulty self-regulating, respecting authority, or experiencing success in school.

3. Neglectful parenting often results in more global dysfunction. These children struggle with self-control, self-esteem, and overall competence.

4. Authoritative parenting tends to result in children who are happy and competent, who respect authority and others, who are able to tolerate distress, and who are disciplined, capable, and successful. Authoritative parents also tend to understand and respect individual differences in child temperament. As a result, these children are able to develop healthy social and emotional health.

## Long-Term Family Goals

1. Parents learn to establish clear expectations and goals.

2. Parents become comfortable allowing input from the children.

3. Communication is frequent, clear, and age-appropriate.

4. Children understand the rules and possible consequences.

5. Parents are nurturing, loving, and understanding.

6. Family develops an understanding of their individual temperament traits and its impact on relationships in and out of the family system.

On the following pages are two parenting style and temperament assignments to give to your clients one week at a time. In session, explain the topic to them using the sample conversation I have provided as a guide, and then describe the assignments to them, answering any questions they may have. If necessary, help the family modify the assignments to make them developmentally appropriate and understandable for all family members. Then send them home with the following assignments over the next two sessions, and process what they learned about their parenting and temperament styles, as well as their experience of sharing about the topic with one another, in each subsequent session.

## Therapist Assignment Summaries

**Assignment #1:** *Parenting Style and Temperament Conversation*

The purpose of this assignment is for the family to explore how parenting and temperament styles impact the family dynamic.

**Assignment #2:** *The Temperament Game for Adolescents and Adults*

The purpose of this assignment is for family members to identify their likely temperament style. They will then discuss how true this feels to them and give one another input as well.

Once your clients have completed both the parenting style and the temperament assignments, and you have processed each in session, review the following goals to solidify their new understanding of this important topic.

## Parenting and Temperament Styles Assignments Wrap-Up

"Now that you have done both the parenting styles and the temperament assignments, and we have talked about them in session, let's see what you have learned. Do you feel that you..."

1. (Parents) Understand the differences between the four parenting styles?
2. (Parents) Have made any shifts in your parenting style?
3. Have identified your individual temperament styles?
4. Are more committed to respecting your individual temperament styles?
5. Are a little closer and more connected as a family after spending two weeks learning about parenting styles and temperaments?

## Sample Conversation

We are going to be talking about parenting styles and individual temperaments over the next couple of weeks. Parenting style has a great impact on how you discipline, communicate, and nurture connection and closeness with your children. Temperament refers to the basic personality that you are born with. It also affects how active, emotional, sensitive, and social you are, so it's important to know and respect the similarities and differences between your individual temperament traits.

There are four temperament styles: sanguine, choleric, melancholic, and phlegmatic. Sanguine children are enthusiastic, active, social, talkative, charismatic, extroverted, outgoing, and risk-seeking. Choleric children are short-tempered, fast, irritable, extroverted, independent, decisive, goal-oriented, and ambitious. They also tend to be natural leaders. Melancholic children are analytical, wise, quiet, detail-oriented, introverted, self-reliant, reserved, thoughtful, often anxious, and perfectionistic. They are usually deep thinkers and feelers. Finally, phlegmatic children are relaxed, peaceful, quiet, easygoing, sympathetic, caring, accommodating, and reserved. In young children, these temperaments are also often described as easy, difficult, and slow to warm up.

Temperament affects parenting, as children with different temperaments often respond differently to different parenting techniques. For instance, a sanguine/easy child is likely to be excited about new activities, make friends easily, and tell you all about it afterward, while a melancholic/slow-to-warm-up child may prefer to stay home, worry before the activity, and keep to themselves.

If a parent becomes impatient with the melancholic child and compares that child to the sanguine/easy child, the melancholic child is likely to feel that they are not allowed to feel the way they do, which may injure self-esteem and possibly even create resentment toward the "easier" sibling.

Just as there are four temperament styles, there are four parenting styles:

1. *Authoritarian/Disciplinarian*
   This style is a very strict, with many rules that are generally not explained to the child. There is very little communication, punishment is common, there's not much nurturing, and there are very high expectations. Children of authoritarian parents tend to be obedient, but they are less happy and less socially confident, and they often lack self-esteem.

2. *Permissive/Indulgent*

This style has limited or no rules and minimal expectations. Parents with this style are generally warm and nurturing, and they communicate openly, but they offer little direction, leaving the children to figure things out. Children of permissive parents tend to have difficulty self-regulating, respecting authority, or experiencing success in school.

3. *Neglectful/Uninvolved*

Parents with this style don't tend to do much in the way of discipline, don't communicate often, offer very little nurturing, and have few expectations. Children of neglectful and involved parents tend to have very little self-control, self-esteem, discipline, or general competence.

4. *Authoritative*

This style offers appropriate discipline, with clear rules and explanations. There tends to be frequent, age-appropriate communication and regular nurturing. Parents set high, yet reasonable, expectations and goals, and they allow their children to have input.

> **Authoritative parenting tends to result in children who are happy and competent overall, who respect authority and others, who are able to tolerate distress, and who are disciplined, capable, and successful.**

# Questions to Explore with Family Members

1. Do you think the rules and consequences are pretty clear in our family?

   _____

   _____

2. Do we communicate fairly regularly?

   _____

   _____

3. What sort of expectations do we have in our home?

   _____

   _____

4. Do the expectations feel high but fair?

   _____

   _____

5. Children, do you feel like you are allowed to have some input regarding the rules and expectations?

   _____

   _____

6. Does it make sense that we might have different temperaments and personality styles?

   _____

   _____

I'm going to send you home today with one of two parenting style and temperament assignments that are going to benefit you in three ways:

1. First, you are going to have a family conversation about parenting and temperament styles.

2. Next, you are going to learn more about healthy parenting and how your temperament style makes you unique.

3. And finally, by exploring your parenting and temperament styles, you are going to strengthen your connection and sense of being on the same team.

*Always remember to be loving and respectful!*

# Parenting and Temperament Conversation

*Everything depends on upbringing.*
—Leo Tolstoy

Enjoy a nice conversation about the parenting and temperament styles in your family. Choose one person as the family secretary to take notes about the family responses. Then take turns asking the following questions. Go around the family one by one, answering each question according to how you feel. Remember to always be honest, kind, respectful, and loving.

1. Do you think that the rules and consequences are clear in our family?

_____

_____

_____

2. Do you think that you have very few, too many, or a reasonable amount of expectations put on you?

_____

_____

_____

3. Children, when you are punished for things, do you usually understand why? Parents, when you punish your child, do you explain the reasons for the punishment?

_____

_____

_____

4. Do you feel like we have a good balance of expectations, affection, and fun in our family?

_____

_____

_____

5. Children, do you feel like you have a say about family rules and consequences? Parents, do you give your child a say in family rules and consequences?

_____

_____

_____

6. Children, do you think it's important to treat parents, teachers, and other authority figures with respect?

_____

_____

_____

7. Children, do you feel like you can speak up if something doesn't seem fair, or do you worry about what will happen if you don't obey right away? Parents, do you respectfully allow your child to speak up if something doesn't seem fair?

_____

_____

_____

8. Do you feel like you are accepted for who you are in this family?

_____

_____

_____

9. Is there anything else you think we could do as a family to be closer, more respectful, or clearer about the rules and expectations?

_____

_____

_____

# The Temperament Game for Adolescents and Adults

Fold the right side of this piece of paper so the numbers are hidden. Then put a check mark beside the statements that apply to you.

| | |
|---|---|
| _____ I get very excited about new opportunities. | 1 |
| _____ People often don't know how I'm feeling. | 4 |
| _____ I enjoy spending time alone. | 3 |
| _____ I like to be in charge. | 2 |
| _____ I tend to be very chatty. | 1 |
| _____ I like having goals. | 2 |
| _____ I really feel for people when they are sad. | 4 |
| _____ I like things to be organized and in order. | 3 |
| _____ I don't find it difficult to compromise. | 4 |
| _____ I find it pretty easy to make decisions. | 2 |
| _____ I like to be on the go. | 1 |
| _____ I enjoy being quiet and deep in thought. | 3 |
| _____ I tend to have a short temper. | 2 |
| _____ I really enjoy being around others. | 1 |
| _____ I like to do things well and not be sloppy. | 3 |
| _____ I'm pretty easygoing. | 4 |
| _____ I have lots of friends. | 1 |
| _____ I do things pretty quickly. | 2 |
| _____ I often feel anxious. | 3 |
| _____ It takes a lot to upset me. | 4 |

Next, open the paper and write the number of 1s you have in the #1 square, the number of 2s in the #2 square, the number of 3s in the #3 square, and the number of 4s in the #4 square. Whatever square you have the highest number in tells you your temperament, though it is common to have a combination of temperaments.

| #1 MELANCHOLIC | #2 CHOLERIC |
|---|---|
| *I am…* | *I am…* |
| Analytical | Decisive |
| Wise | Natural leader |
| Quiet/reserved | Fast |
| Detail-oriented | Short-tempered |
| Deep thinker/feeler | Irritable |
| Introverted | Extroverted |
| Anxious | Independent |
| Perfectionistic | Goal-oriented |

| #3 MELANCHOLIC | #4 PHLEGMATIC |
|---|---|
| *I am…* | *I am…* |
| Relaxed | Enthusiastic |
| Peaceful/quiet | Active |
| Introverted | Social |
| Easygoing | Talkative |
| Sympathetic | Charismatic |
| Caring | Extroverted |
| Hides emotions | Outgoing |
| Can compromise | Risk-seeking |

Finally, take turns reading the details of your temperament style to your family, and talk about how true it feels to you and the rest of your family.

"My temperament type is… which means I am…"

Keep in mind that these are general descriptions. Your adolescent may have some or all of these traits, and they may change as they grow older.

# 7

# Self-Esteem and Compassion

## Therapist Preparation

A client's level of self-esteem directly impacts their psychological health, identity, assertiveness, and belief that they are worthy of love and are "enough." Many factors can affect self-esteem, such as trauma, abuse, bullying, gender, race, and sexual orientation, but the initial impact is determined by an individual's experience in their family of origin.

Studies of young children have shown that the parenting style they experience in the first few years of life has the greatest impact on the initial development of self-esteem and the subsequent beliefs, assumptions, schemas, and thought processes the child internalizes. From there, a circular experience develops wherein a child's life circumstances shape and/or alter their self-esteem, and self-esteem shapes and/or alters their life choices and circumstances.

If children grow up in a home where they feel loved and valued for who they are, they may still struggle with situational self-esteem challenges at times, but they will feel good about themselves overall. If they instead experience physical or emotional abuse or neglect, they are more likely to develop a characterological self-esteem problem.

As clinicians, it is our job to help the family create an environment that nurtures healthy self-esteem. You can do so by first addressing the health of the parents' self-esteem and examining the ways they may or may not be fostering healthy self-esteem in their children. Helping parents model and teach self-acceptance, compassion, encouragement, respect, boundaries, realistic expectations, assertiveness, and vulnerability will allow all family members to begin to love and value themselves and one another for who they are, as well as create a life of meaning and purpose, free from fear.

## The Impact of Low Self-Esteem on the Family System

1. Attention is focused on family member struggling with anxiety and depression.
2. Communication challenges due to a family member's difficulty with assertiveness and decision-making.
3. Limited family activities due to a family member's difficulty trying new things.
4. Tension in the home due to a family member's difficulty with feedback.
5. Family members may feel inadequate due to another's perfectionism.
6. Family cohesion may be disrupted due to a family member's poor relationship choices.
7. Individuals may feel hurt or disrespected due to a family member's lack of appropriate boundaries

## Long-Term Family Goals

1. Family encourages assertiveness and independent decision making.
2. Family models acceptance and compassion.
3. Family focuses on effort, not perfection.
4. Parents models how to maintain healthy boundaries.
5. Parents maintain an awareness of self-esteem challenges in children.
6. Parents help children reframe any negative narratives.
7. Family members avoid making comparisons.
8. Family members practice self-care and self-love.

On the following pages are three self-esteem assignments to give to your clients one week at a time. In session, explain the topic to them using the sample conversation I have provided as a guide, and then describe the assignments to them, answering any questions they may have. If necessary, help the family modify the assignments to make them developmentally appropriate and understandable for all family members. Then send them home with the following assignments over the next three sessions, and process what they learned about self-esteem, as well as their experience of sharing about the topic with one another, in each subsequent session.

## Therapist Assignment Summaries

**Assignment #1:** *Self-Esteem Conversation*

The purpose of this assignment is for family members to explore their own self-esteem and how it has been impacted by the family dynamic.

**Assignment #2:** *What I Like about Myself*

The purpose of this assignment is for family members to focus on what they like about themselves and one another. It gives them an opportunity to validate their strengths and to bond with one another by sharing compliments.

**Assignment #3:** *Self-Esteem Collage*

The purpose of this assignment is to help family members develop healthy self-esteem by creating a collage of their individual strengths, identities, and dreams. By sharing their collage with family members, they can each appreciate their individual personalities and strengths.

Once your clients have completed all three of the self-esteem and compassion assignments, and you have processed each in session, review the following goals to solidify their new understanding of this very important topic.

## Self-Esteem Assignments Wrap-Up

"Now that you have done all three self-esteem assignments, and we have talked about them in session, let's see what you have learned. Do you feel that you..."

1. Understand how important it is to acknowledge the things you like about yourself?
2. Believe that it is more important to focus on effort and learning than on being perfect?

3. Understand that everyone is different, with a unique personality, strengths, likes, dislikes, and dreams?

4. Understand that it is important to love yourself for who you are and not compare yourselves to others?

5. Understand that it is important to be accepting and compassionate to yourselves and one another?

6. Are a little closer and more connected as a family after spending three weeks learning about self-esteem?

## Sample Conversation

Over the next few weeks we are going to focus on self-esteem. Most of us are familiar with the importance of healthy self-esteem, but we don't necessarily understand what that really means. There are three types of self-esteem: high, low, and inflated. Having high self-esteem means that you are really sure of your own worth and your abilities. This is important because it has such an impact on the choices and decisions you make in your life.

People with low self-esteem don't really feel that they deserve to be treated well or that they are capable of achieving things. This often gets in the way of their even trying to accomplish things. They sometimes have trouble being assertive, and they may let others make important decisions for them.

People with inflated self-esteem think they are better than other people. They overestimate their own worth and underestimate the worth of others, which doesn't tend to make them very likable.

If you have high self-esteem, you are more likely to try new things, give your best effort at work and school, and surround yourself with friends who treat you with respect. You may even cope better with disappointment or failure because you like yourself enough to not think of yourself as a disappointment or a failure. Many of us struggle with low self-esteem in certain areas of life, and the great thing is that it can absolutely be improved.

# Questions to Explore with Family Members

1. On a scale of 1–10, with 1 being the lowest and 10 being the highest, how much would you say you like yourself?

   _____

   _____

2. Are you able to make your own decisions most of the time, or do you usually need others to make them for you?

   _____

   _____

3. Is it okay to share your opinion about things in your family?

   _____

   _____

4. Do you think it's important that your friends treat you respectfully?

   _____

   _____

5. Children, do you think you have to get an A on every assignment and test, or is it okay to get a B if you gave it your best effort?

   _____

   _____

6. Is your family good at giving one another compliments?

   _____

   _____

I'm going to send you home today with one of three self-esteem assignments that are going to benefit you in three ways:

1. First, you are going to have a nice family conversation about the importance of healthy self-esteem and compassion.

2. Next, you are going to learn to identify the things you like about yourself and one another.

3. And finally, you are going to see how worthy you are of loving yourself and your own unique personality, interests, talents, and dreams.

*Always remember to be loving and respectful!*

# Self-Esteem and Compassion Conversation

*You, yourself, as much as anybody in the entire universe, deserve your love and affection.*
—Sharon Salzberg

Enjoy a nice conversation about self-esteem and compassion. Choose one person as the family secretary to take notes about the family responses. Then take turns asking the following questions. Go around the family one by one, answering each question according to how you feel. Remember to always be honest, kind, respectful, and loving.

1. Do you think you are ever too hard on yourself?

_____

_____

_____

2. Do you think we pay one another enough compliments?

_____

_____

_____

3. Children, do you feel like we expect you to be perfect, or is your best effort good enough?

_____

_____

_____

4. Do you feel accepted for who you are?

_____

_____

_____

5. Are you able to be kind to yourself when you are having a tough time?

_____

_____

_____

6. Do you think we are good at showing one another kindness and compassion?

_____

_____

_____

7. Are we good at relaxing, or do we always have to be productive?

_____

_____

_____

8. Do you think we allow one another to say what is on our mind?

_____

_____

_____

9. Do you think it's important to not compare yourself to others?

_____

_____

_____

10. Is there anything else we can do as a family to help develop healthy self-esteem?

_____

_____

_____

# What I Like about Myself

Take a few moments to complete the following sentences, and then take turns sharing them with the family.

1.  Something I really like about my physical appearance is... (e.g., my smile, my eyes, my hair)

    _____

    _____

    _____

2.  Something I really like about how I relate to others is.... (e.g., that I'm fun, caring, a good listener)

    _____

    _____

    _____

3.  Something I really like about my personality is... (e.g., that I'm responsible, organized, funny)

    _____

    _____

    _____

4.  Something I think I'm talented at is... (e.g., playing the piano, drawing, singing)

    _____

    _____

    _____

5.  Something I'm really proud of is... (e.g., being a good friend, my artwork, my attitude)

    _____

    _____

    _____

Now complete the following sentences for each family member.

1. Something I really like about your physical appearance is...

_____

_____

_____

2. Something I really like about how you relate to others is...

_____

_____

_____

3. Something I really like about your personality is...

_____

_____

_____

4. Something I think you are really talented at is...

_____

_____

_____

5. Something that makes me really proud of you is...

_____

_____

_____

# Self-Esteem Collage

**Materials:**

- Large piece of poster board for each family member

- Magazines

- Scissors

- Glue

Tear or cut out pictures that represent YOU from various magazines. Use any pictures that represent your personality, talents, hobbies, friends, dreams, and so forth, and glue them onto the poster board in any way that appeals to you.

When you are done, show your collage to your family, and share what these pictures mean to you.

Have a conversation about things you learned from seeing each person's collage.

# 8

# Boundaries and Discipline

## Therapist Preparation

Healthy boundaries are essential to a healthy family system. They allow the various subsystems to be nurtured, and they guide expectations, limits, and consequences. These boundaries are often unwritten rules that define family interactions, and they separate what is allowed from what is not.

In my private practice, I use a set of Russian nesting dolls to illustrate the importance of boundaries in the family system. At the core is the individual who needs and deserves time for self-care, personal development, social connections, and other aspects of being a unique human being. Next is the couple subsystem, which also requires privacy for connection, intimacy, and relationship-nurturing. This is followed by the nuclear family, which flourishes when there is time for bonding, communicating, and maintaining rituals and identity. Next is extended family, followed by friends and then community.

It is within the boundaries of the family system, and with the guidance of the parental subsystem, that expectations for discipline develop. Discipline is a practice of training children to obey a code of behavior that shows respect for the family and teaches self-control, patience, and cooperation. On the other hand, children who are neither taught proper discipline, nor respect for boundaries are more likely to struggle with anger and resentment.

It's important that parents understand the difference between diffuse, rigid, and healthy boundaries.

**Diffuse boundaries:** When a family system has diffuse boundaries the rules and expectations are often unclear and inconsistent. There may be little supervision and communication, or over-involvement in one another's lives. These weak boundaries may result in entitlement, lack of respect for rules, or feelings of being smothered by others that do not respect their privacy.

**Rigid boundaries:** A family with rigid boundaries tends to have very strict expectations and rules with little or no flexibility. This type of strong boundary may not allow family members to develop their own identity, question the rules, or feel seen as unique individuals.

**Healthy boundaries:** A family with healthy boundaries, sets clear rules and expectations, has open communication, and allows for input from all members. These flexible boundaries allows all family members to feel seen, heard, and respected, while understanding that ultimately the parents are the final decision-makers.

There are also three general approaches to discipline: preventive, supportive, and corrective. Many parents consider only the corrective aspect when they think of discipline, but it's important to teach them all three so they are more successful in raising children who feel supported and respect boundaries.

1. **Preventive discipline:** This involves clearly communicating rules to children, instilling in them the motivation to cooperate, and setting consequences when they do not.

2. **Supportive discipline:** This involves assisting with any misbehavior so children can get back on track, as opposed to just jumping to a consequence. Sometimes this requires hearing them out, noticing a pattern of why they got off track, and redirecting them.

3. **Corrective discipline:** At this point, the consequence is generally carried out.

Emphasize to parents that they are the role models when it comes to boundaries and discipline. The adage "Do as I say, not as I do" will not work, so parents need to be mindful of their own use of boundaries and self-discipline. It's also crucial that they realize that along with boundaries and discipline, their children need attention, validation, and affirmation. It's important to "catch them doing good," as this encourages positive behavior and can work to prevent the need for discipline.

## The Impact of Lack of Boundaries and Discipline on the Family System

1. One family member's mood impacts the overall family mood.
2. Family subsystems are not properly nurtured.
3. Children don't learn to delay gratification or develop self-control.
4. Family members aren't taught to value self-care.
5. Family members do not differentiate between privacy and secrecy.
6. Rules are not respected.
7. Parents are not respected as authority figures.
8. There is a lack of mutual respect.
9. Rigid boundaries do not allow for negotiation.
10. There is a risk of enmeshment or cutoff.
11. Family members have difficulty cooperating in relationships.
12. Anger and resentment are present.

## Long-Term Family Goals

1. Family members show mutual respect.
2. Parents enjoy a private life with healthy connection and intimacy.
3. Parents do not use children as confidants.
4. There is a balance between engagement and autonomy.
5. Open communication is encouraged.
6. Parents model discipline, cooperation, and consistency.
7. Rules, limits, and consequences are clear and are carried out calmly.
8. Parents "catch the children being good."
9. Parents understand preventive, supportive, and corrective discipline.
10. Parents treat children as individuals and discipline them accordingly.

On the following pages are two boundaries and discipline assignments to give to your clients one week at a time. In session, explain the topic to them using the sample conversation I have provided as a guide, and then describe the assignments to them, answering any questions they may have. If necessary, help the family modify the assignments to make them developmentally appropriate and understandable for all family members. Then send them home with the following assignments over the next two sessions, and process what they learned about boundaries and discipline, as well as their experience of sharing about the topic with one another, in each subsequent session.

## Therapist Assignment Summaries

**Assignment #1:** *Boundaries and Discipline Conversation*

The purpose of this assignment is for family members to explore boundaries and discipline and to understand its impact on the family dynamic.

**Assignment #2:** *Russian Nesting Dolls*

The purpose of this assignment is for family members to focus on what they like about themselves and one another. It gives them an opportunity to validate their strengths and to bond with one another by sharing compliments.

Once your clients have completed both of the boundaries and discipline assignments, and you have processed each in session, review the following goals in order to solidify their new understanding of this important topic.

## Boundaries and Discipline Assignments Wrap-Up

"Now that you have done both of the boundaries and discipline assignments, and we have talked about them in session, let's see what you have learned. Do you feel that you..."

1.  Understand why boundaries are important for you and your family?
2.  (Parents) Will make having couple time a priority?
3.  See how important it is to respect one another's boundaries through your actions and words?
4.  Understand the difference between diffuse, rigid, and healthy boundaries?
5.  Understand the difference between preventive, supportive, and corrective discipline?
6.  Agree that it is important to be clear about the rules and consequences in order to have healthy discipline?
7.  Understand that discipline is not "one size fits all"?
8.  Are a little closer and more connected as a family after spending two weeks working on boundaries and discipline?

## Sample Conversation

Over the next couple of weeks we are going to focus on boundaries and discipline in your family. A boundary is something that separates things, like a fence does, and in a family it is what separates your identity from everyone else's, and it allows you to have your own space and to respect the space of others as well. That means there are times when your parents are going to do things without you, times when you are going to do things with your friends, and times when you are all going to be together. It's important that you all respect one another's boundaries at those times. Boundaries also guide how you treat other people in your family, including what you say to them. If you have healthy boundaries, you treat one another with respect through your words and actions.

Healthy discipline is actually an example of maintaining good boundaries. As children, when you know and respect the rules your parents have set, you are respecting the discipline boundary. In order to do that, though, it's important that your parents make the rules clear and let you know what the consequences are if you don't follow them. Learning to respect and follow the rules in your home actually helps you learn patience, cooperation, and self-control, which will make the rest of your life more manageable.

# Questions to Explore with Family Members

1. Do you think you understand what the rules are in your home?

   _____

   _____

2. Do you think the consequences of rule-breaking are usually fair?

   _____

   _____

3. Are you able to talk to one another about the rules and consequences?

   _____

   _____

4. Do you think you respect one another's boundaries?

   _____

   _____

5. As parents, do you give yourselves permission to do things without the kids sometimes? As children, are you allowed to do things alone or with friends when it is appropriate?

   _____

   _____

6. Do you ask before you use something that belongs to another family member?

   _____

   _____

7. Do you respect one another's privacy?

_____

_____

8. As children, do you respect that your parents have the ultimate authority and are in charge?

_____

_____

I'm going to send you home today with one of two boundaries and discipline assignments that are going to benefit you in three ways:

1. First, you are going to have a conversation about boundaries and discipline in your family.

2. Next, you are going to learn more about healthy boundaries in your life and relationships.

3. Finally, you will learn what healthy boundaries mean to your family members.

*Always remember to be loving and respectful!*

# Boundaries and Discipline Conversation

*You are the bows from which your children as living arrows are sent forth.*
—Khalil Gibran

Enjoy a nice conversation about boundaries and discipline. Choose one person as the family secretary to take notes about the family responses. Then take turns asking the following questions. Go around the family one by one, answering each question according to how you feel. Remember to always be honest, kind, respectful, and loving.

1. What are the different boundaries in our family?

_____

_____

_____

2. Do you think that we respect one another's privacy?

_____

_____

_____

3. Do you think we are respectful of one another's boundaries?

_____

_____

_____

4. Do you understand what the rules are in our home, and do they seem to be fair?

_____

_____

_____

5. Do we all know what the consequences are when we break a rule or don't do something we are told to do?

_____

_____

_____

6. Do you understand how learning to respect boundaries and discipline helps you at school, work, with friends, and so on?

_____

_____

_____

7. Children, are there any rules that you think are unfair?

_____

_____

_____

8. Children, do you feel like you can talk to your parents about the rules? Parents, do you allow your children to discuss the rules with you?

_____

_____

_____

# Russian Nesting Doll Assignment

For this assignment, you will explore the different boundaries in your life. The doll in the center is you, the next represents your parents, the third is your extended family, the fourth is your friends, and the fifth is your community.

Write a few words in each circle to describe what you think makes that boundary healthy.

**Examples:**

Me: some time alone for hobbies and self-care

Parents: date night, kids knock on bedroom door

Extended family: holidays spent together, ask before plans are made

Friends: time with friends apart from family/spouse

Community: volunteer work

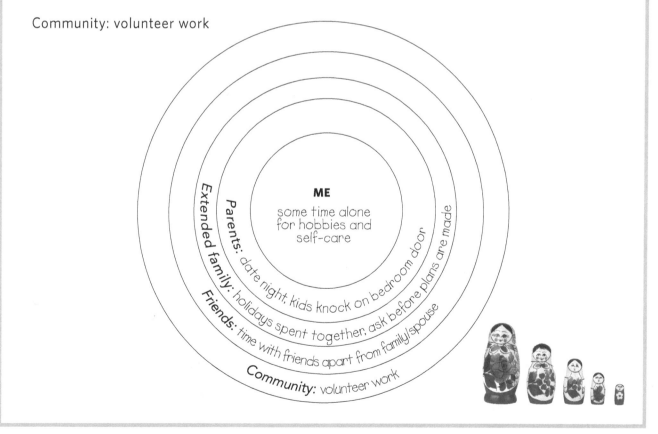

# Russian Nesting Doll Assignment

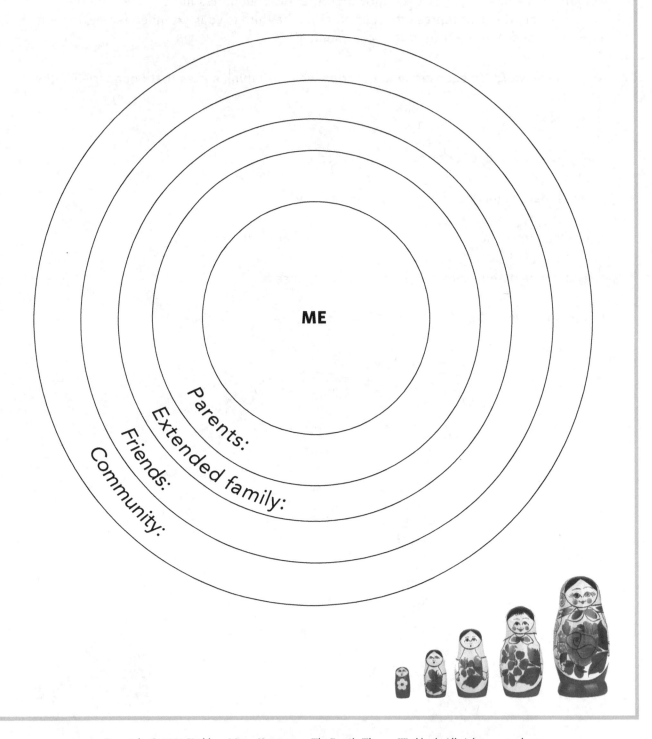

ME

Parents:

Extended family:

Friends:

Community:

# 9

# Sibling Love/Sibling Rivalry

## Therapist Preparation

According to the renowned Austrian psychologist Alfred Adler, all siblings "strive for significance." Though they generally love one another, they also compete to define themselves as individuals and to be seen, heard, valued, and validated by their parents.

If children feel they are receiving unequal amounts of attention, discipline, and responsiveness from their parents, they are more likely to become angry, resentful, jealous, and even vengeful with their siblings. According to British psychologist Judith Dunn, children are sensitive to differences in treatment by their parents as young as age 1, understand family rules by 18 months, and are able to adapt themselves to the family dynamics by the age of 3.

Research also indicates that siblings are most competitive between the ages of 10 and 15, and even one-third of adults describe their relationship with their siblings as distant and full of rivalry. Fortunately, these feelings tend to diminish over time, and 80 percent of adults over age 60 report close ties with their siblings ... so there is always hope.

In order to prevent unhealthy sibling rivalry, parents need to avoid any favoritism and be sensitive to the impact of birth order, the arrival of a new baby, and the impact of a child with a disability or chronic illness. In addition, parents should respect individual personality and temperament. Moments of rivalry and bickering are to be expected, and parents should never ask children to "stuff down" their feelings. Instead, they should encourage children to express their concerns, and they should respond with active listening and empathy. When parents manage conflicts in a healthy way, siblings are able to truly enjoy these first peer relationships and learn to practice assertiveness, sharing, caring, and negotiation.

We can help our parents minimize sibling rivalry by encouraging the following behaviors:

1. Treat their children as unique individuals.
2. Reassure their children when they feel things are unfair and explain their decisions.
3. Explain to children how their age affects rules about bedtime, curfews, and so forth, which may differ between siblings.
4. Have one-on-one "special time" with each child. If parents spend even 20 minutes doing whatever the child chooses, this can have a tremendous impact on bonding and making the child feel special.
5. Encourage cooperation, not competition.
6. Allow children to have some alone time and a space of their own.

7. When children are calm, let them express their complaints about a sibling while also encouraging them to share something positive.

8. Avoid comparing or labeling children.

9. Encourage teamwork.

10. Teach positive ways to ask for attention.

11. Catch them being good.

12. Teach problem-solving skills, negotiation skills, and emotional intelligence.

## The Impact of Unhealthy Sibling Rivalry on the Family System

1. Conflict may become more physically, intellectually, and emotionally hurtful as children become adolescents.

2. Parents and children experience stress and tension.

3. Hostility increases in families that don't allow fighting while also not offering a productive way to communicate and repair.

4. Rivalry may become abusive, which presents as a long-term pattern of hostility and involves secrecy and an imbalance of power.

5. The goal becomes domination and humiliation.

6. Family cutoffs develop.

## Long-Term Family Goals

1. Sibling conflicts are isolated to particular incidents and are reciprocal, occasional, visible to others, and age-appropriate.

2. Each child feels like they receive equal attention and responsiveness, and they feel like discipline is fair.

3. Each child feels significant, appreciated, and valued for their individual identity.

4. Parents listen well and offer alternative ways to manage conflicts.

5. Parents promote cooperation, not competition.

6. Parents spend one-on-one time with children, avoid comparisons, and encourage teamwork.

7. Siblings are permitted to share complaints while also validating positive traits.

8. Children are allowed to have their own personal space and privacy.

9. Siblings develop a wonderful first peer relationship through which they learn to navigate life relationships, come to intuitively understand one another, and enjoy an unmatched connection as they grow older.

On the following pages are two sibling love/sibling rivalry assignments to give to your clients one week at a time. In session, explain the topic to them using the sample conversation I have provided as a guide, and then describe the assignments to them, answering any questions they may have. If necessary, help the family modify the assignments to make them developmentally appropriate and understandable for all family members. Then send them home with the following assignments over the next two sessions, and process what they learned about sibling relationships, as well as their experience of sharing about the topic with one another, in each subsequent session.

## Therapist Assignment Summaries

**Assignment #1**: *Sibling Love/Sibling Rivalry Conversation*

The purpose of this assignment is for siblings to explore their relationships and for parents to learn healthy methods of creating and maintaining healthy sibling relationships.

**Assignment #2**: *Sibling Love/Sibling Rivalry Perception Quiz*

The purpose of this assignment is for family members to learn about one another and to see one another as unique individuals. First, each child will write their responses to each statement. Then they will take turns asking their family members to guess their responses to each statement to see who knows them the most. Some of the questions are more sensitive in nature and must be treated respectfully and delicately.

Once your clients have completed both of the sibling love/sibling rivalry assignments, and you have processed each in session, review the following goals to solidify their new understanding of this important topic.

## Sibling Love/Sibling Rivalry Assignments Wrap-Up

"Now that you have done both of the sibling love/sibling rivalry assignments, and we have talked about them in session, let's see what you have learned. Do you feel that you..."

Children:

1. Appreciate your siblings' positive traits?
2. Are allowed to have some alone time and have your own special space?
3. Know that it's normal to have some conflicts with your siblings but that you should never purposefully embarrass or hurt them?
4. Know that your parents listen to you when you are upset with your siblings and help you to find a solution?
5. Feel blessed to know that your sibling relationships will be the longest relationships in your life?

Parents:

6. Show equal attention and responsiveness to each child?
7. Listen well to your children and allow them to share complaints while also encouraging cooperation?
8. Understand the signs of unhealthy sibling rivalry?
9. See the importance of having some one-on-one time with each child, avoiding comparisons, and encouraging teamwork?

All:

10. Have learned more about one another's likes, dislikes, worries, hopes, and dreams?
11. Are a little closer and more connected as a family after spending two weeks working on sibling rivalry/sibling love?

## Sample Conversation

Over the next few weeks we are going to talk about the sibling relationships in your family. Though you all love one another, I'm sure there are times when you don't get along. It's perfectly normal to be irritated with one another at times or to have an argument, but we also want to make sure that you are able to resolve things and not hurt one another in any way.

You all need to feel heard, to know that you are important, and to feel like you are allowed to be yourself. It's also important to know that because you are all different people and different ages, sometimes things like bedtime, curfew, and consequences will be a little different, but we never want you to feel like things are unfair.

Parents, to maintain healthy sibling relationships among your children, it's important that you really listen to your children when they are upset and that you help them find a way to cooperate with one another. They should never have to stuff down their feelings. Instead, they should feel like you hear them, empathize with them, and can help them find a way to problem solve, negotiate, and be caring while they do so.

Believe it or not, our longest relationships are usually with our siblings. Parents, the more you make your children feel valued for who they are (avoiding any favoritism), spend special one-on-one time with them, avoid comparisons or labeling, and allow them to express their feelings, the closer they will be as siblings now and as they grow older. That will make this relationship their most special relationship.

# Questions to Explore with Family Members

1. On a scale of 1–10, with 1 being the worst and 10 being the best, how well do you think you get along with your siblings?

   _____

   _____

2. Children, are you allowed to express your anger, and do your parents help you to resolve it?

   _____

   _____

3. Children, do you ever have time alone in a space that is just for you?

   _____

   _____

4. Parents, do you see your children as true individuals and avoid comparisons?

   _____

   _____

5. Do you all agree that when siblings have a conflict they should never embarrass, harass, or demean one another?

   _____

   _____

6. Parents, are you able to take turns spending 20 minutes or so a week alone with each child to do something of their choice?

   _____

   _____

7. Can you each say three things you like about your sibling right now?

_____

_____

I'm going to send you home today with one of two sibling love/sibling rivalry assignments that are going to benefit you in three ways:

1.  First, you are going to have a nice family conversation about your sibling relationships.

2.  Next, you are going to learn more about how your parents can help you to have normal, healthy sibling rivalry without being hurtful.

3.  And finally, you are going to see how important your relationship with your siblings is now and how important it will be forever.

*Always remember to be loving and respectful!*

# Sibling Love/Sibling Rivalry Conversation

*Brother and sister, together as friends, ready to face whatever life sends.*

—Robert Brault

Enjoy a nice conversation about sibling love and sibling rivalry. Choose one person as the family secretary to take notes about the family responses. Then take turns asking the following questions. Go around the family one by one, answering each question according to how you feel. Remember always to be honest, kind, respectful, and loving.

1.  What does it mean to you to be a sister or a brother?

_____

_____

_____

2.  When do you have the most fun with your siblings?

_____

_____

_____

3.  What makes you the angriest with your sibling?

_____

_____

_____

4. What helps you when you are angry?

_____

_____

_____

5. Children, do you think your parents treat you all fairly?

_____

_____

_____

6. Children, do you feel that your parents appreciate and value you for who you are?

_____

_____

_____

7. Children, would you like more one-on-one time with your parents?

_____

_____

_____

8. Children, do you have a space that is just for you and your things?

_____

_____

_____

9. Children, are your parents helpful when you and your siblings argue?

_____

_____

_____

10. Do you ever say or do things to your siblings that you later regret? Are you able to apologize?

_____

_____

_____

11. What is your favorite thing about each of your siblings?

_____

_____

_____

12. Do you realize that your relationships with your siblings are usually the longest relationships in your life? Isn't that cool.

_____

_____

_____

# Sibling Perception Quiz

Begin by completing each of these sentences. Some will be easy to complete, and others will take some thought and time. When you are all ready, take turns asking your siblings to complete the sentences as they pertain to you to see who knows you the most and to help them learn more about you. Sharing your responses will help you all to see one another as separate individuals with your own likes, dislikes, anxieties, perceptions, hopes, and dreams.

1. My favorite color is _____.

2. My favorite food is _____.

3. My favorite season is _____.

4. My favorite holiday is _____.

5. My favorite movie is _____.

6. My favorite flower is _____.

7. Am I a night owl or an early bird? _____.

8. My best friend is _____.

9. One of the happiest times in my life has been _____.

10. One of the saddest times in my life has been _____.

11. It hurts my feelings when _____.

12. My most positive traits are _____.

13. I am hardest on myself about _____.

14. My favorite subject in school is _____.

15. What I would like most in life is _____.

16. My dream career would be _____.

17. I get anxious when _____.

18. I get angry when _____.

19. The thing I love most about my siblings is _____.

20. My dream for us as siblings is _____.

part 2

# Unique Family Challenges

# 10

# Coping with Grief

## Therapist Preparation

Clients may grieve many different things, including relationship breakups, job losses, or physical losses due to an illness or accident, but for the purpose of this chapter I will focus on grief due to the death of a loved one.

When working with families on issues related to grief, it is important to understand the common emotional and physical effects of grief and to individualize treatment to your client's specific needs. The loss of a loved one is traumatic, and it is even more severe when a parent experiences the death of a child or a child experiences the death of a parent. These losses rock their very foundation, sense of self, and ability to see a future at all. As always, we must be able to be present with the client, to offer them a safe haven to experience and share their feelings, and to guide them through their individual grief process at their own speed.

Grief is a nonlinear journey, and it can be more complicated for some than for others. It is essential that as psychotherapists, we assess for any preexisting psychopathology or resulting psychopathology and that we make referrals for psychiatric or medical assessments as necessary.

Most of us are familiar with the five stages of grief developed by Elisabeth Kübler-Ross, MD, and I have found these stages helpful when working with grieving clients. Although these stages are a guideline of typical responses that your clients may experience when grieving, it is important to note that there is no "typical response," nor should the client believe they "should" move through the process in a specific manner.

## Five Stages of Grief

1. **Denial:** This helps the individual survive the loss and the sense that life is meaningless and overwhelming. It is nature's way of letting in only what that person can cope with, and it will gradually subside and allow feelings to surface.
2. **Anger:** This is often a reaction to feeling abandoned by the loved one, and it is an emotion that can ground a person temporarily as they gradually begin to experience other emotions that will surface.
3. **Bargaining:** These are the thoughts of "what if…" and "if only…" that a person experiences as they desperately want life to return to what it was.
4. **Depression:** The grief now becomes very present. Life feels like a fog of sadness, and isolation often occurs. It is a necessary step toward acceptance.
5. **Acceptance:** Although the loss does not feel okay, the individual is able to accept that their loved one is physically gone and can begin to move toward a new normal.

In addition to these five stages, David Kessler, who coauthored *On Grief and Grieving* with Elisabeth Kübler-Ross, discovered a sixth stage—meaning:

6. **Meaning:** In his book *Finding Meaning*, Kessler helps those grieving to move from a place of suffering, to a place of honoring the memory of their loved one and finding a sense of meaning in what they have lost.

I also find the four tasks of mourning, as outlined by J. W. Worden, PhD, in his book *Grief Counseling and Grief Therapy*, to be helpful with clients:

1. Accept the reality of loss.
2. Work through the pain of grief.
3. Adjust to life without the deceased.
4. Maintain a connection to the deceased while moving on with life.

Also helpful is the Dual Process Model of Coping with Bereavement, which was developed by Margaret Stroebe, PhD, and Hank Schut, PhD:

1. **Loss-Oriented Process:** At this stage, the client is coping with the actual loss. Behaviors may include crying, yearning, sadness, denial, anger, dwelling on the circumstances of the death, and avoiding restoration activities.
2. **Restoration-Oriented Process:** At this stage, the client is moving toward accepting the loss and developing a new norm. Behaviors may include managing changes in routine, developing new ways of connecting with family and friends, and cultivating a new way of life.

Once again, keep in mind that these stages are not linear, nor will all clients necessarily experience them.

## The Impact of Grief on the Family System

1. The loss of this loved one can serve as a trigger for previous losses.
2. One or more family members may have difficulty with sleep, appetite, and focus.
3. One or more family members may experience irritability.
4. The family may be characterized by feelings of disconnection.
5. Complicated grief:
   a. Following the death of a child:
      - Parents may struggle with post-traumatic stress disorder (PTSD), guilt, and overprotectiveness of other children.
      - Sibling roles may shift, and children may struggle with guilt.
   b. Following the death of a parent:
      - There may be a shift in family roles as one adult remains as the single parent.
      - Children may experience possible PTSD and guilt.
      - Children may exhibit anxiety and fear loss of the surviving parent.
      - Financial stress may occur.

## Long-Term Family Goals

1. Family members normalize and validate one another's feelings.
2. Surviving family members understand the stages of grief.
3. Each family member shares their grief story.
4. Family members develop and practice coping skills, self-care routines, and rituals.
5. Family has a clear and healthy understanding regarding the impact of this loss on familial roles and expectations.
6. Family members allow themselves to be happy and look toward the future.

On the following pages are three coping with grief assignments to give to your clients one week at a time. In session, explain the topic to them using the sample conversation I have provided as a guide, and then describe the assignments to them, answering any questions they may have. If necessary, help the family modify the assignments to make them developmentally appropriate and understandable for all family members. Then send them home with the following assignments over the next three sessions, and process what they learned about grief, as well as their experience of sharing about the topic with one another, in each subsequent session.

## Therapist Assignment Summaries

**Assignment #1:** *Coping with Grief Conversation*

The questions in this conversation will help guide family members to express their feelings about the death of their loved one. It will address unresolved feelings and coping skills and will serve as a reminder that they are supported by one another. Feel free to adjust or add questions as seems appropriate.

**Assignment #2:** *A Letter to Your Loved One*

The purpose of this assignment is to allow each family member to communicate their feelings and pain to the loved one they have lost. Family members should be able to share without fear of judgment, and responses can remain private if they prefer. They should be encouraged to express any feelings they have without guilt or shame.

**Assignment #3:** *Creating a Ritual*

The purpose of this assignment is to help family members feel connected to their loved one while also developing a new normal between rituals. It will assist clients in letting go of any fear of forgetting their loved one or guilt about finding acceptance and moving forward.

Once your clients have completed all three of the coping with grief assignments, and you have processed each in session, review the following goals to solidify their new understanding of this important topic.

## Coping with Grief Assignments Wrap-Up

"Now that you have done all three of the coping with grief assignments, and we have talked about them in session, we are going to review some of what you learned. Do you feel that you…"

1. Were each able to express your experience of the death and how it has affected you?
2. Understand the stages of grief?
3. Have been able to let go of any guilt or blame regarding the death of your loved one?

4. Have developed coping skills to help you deal with any residual difficult feelings?

5. Know what to do to self-soothe when necessary?

6. Have developed rituals individually and as a family?

7. (If applicable for parents) Are able to keep from being overprotective of the children?

8. (If applicable for children) Are able to avoid taking on adult responsibilities?

9. Are able to ask for help when you need it?

10. Are allowing yourselves to have moments of happiness and laughter?

## Sample Conversation

(As with all the sample conversations in this workbook, please use this as a template, and modify as appropriate for your particular clients.)

I'm so sorry that you have all suffered this terrible loss, and I am so grateful that you have come in here for help with the many feelings I'm sure you're having. I want you to know that this is a safe space to talk about whatever is on your mind or to just to listen as others share. There is no one way to move through grief and no absolute timeline either.

I also want you to know that you may experience all sorts of feelings, and some of them may even be feelings that are uncomfortable. It's important that you not have any guilt about any thoughts or feelings you have. Your mind and heart are going to try to make sense of this, and that may mean that sometimes you are angry, sometimes you are sad, sometimes you are anxious, and sometimes you might not feel anything at all. It's all okay.

What's important is that you are able to feel connected to one another, to feel safe to share whatever is on your mind, and to take care of yourself as well.

# Questions to Explore with Family Members

1. Have you been able to talk about your loss?

_____

_____

2. How did it feel when you did?

_____

_____

3. Is there anything in particular that helps when you are feeling very sad?

_____

_____

4. Is there anything that you need to help you with your grief?

_____

_____

I'm going to send you home today with one of three coping with grief assignments that are going to benefit you in three ways:

1. First, it is going to give you an opportunity to talk together about the loss of [*your loved one*] and to feel connected and supported by one another.

2. Next, you are going to have a chance to write a letter to your loved one. You're going to be able to say whatever is on your mind and in your heart, and it will help you to still feel a special connection to them.

3. And finally, you are going to create some rituals that you can do together or on your own, which will also help you soothe your feelings and feel that special connection to your loved one.

*Remember that you all are allowed to have the feelings you have.*
*Be kind and loving to one another.*

# Coping with Grief Conversation

*One often calms one's grief by recounting it.*
—Pierre Corneille

Create a comforting environment where you can have a difficult but important conversation about your experience of death and grief. Make sure everyone is comfortable, turn your phones off, light a candle, and take a moment to close your eyes, take a few deep breaths, and then be present. You may choose a family member to take some notes or simply just talk and listen. Remember to be sensitive toward one another as you have this conversation, and respect that you have each had your own unique experience of this loss.

1. What are you feeling in this moment?

_____

_____

_____

2. Where are you feeling it in your body?

_____

_____

_____

3. Is there any particular part of the day that is most difficult for you?

_____

_____

_____

4. What stages of grief do you think you have already felt? (Denial, anger, bargaining, depression, acceptance)

_____

_____

_____

5. Are you struggling with any feelings of guilt, blame, or responsibility?

_____

_____

_____

6. Do you have any questions about the death that you need to have answered?

_____

_____

_____

7. Is there anything in particular that helps you to feel better when you are having a really difficult moment?

_____

_____

_____

8. Is there anything you need from us to help you?

_____

_____

_____

9. What are your fondest memories of your loved one?

_____

_____

_____

10. If you could have one more day with your loved one, what would you do together?

_____

_____

_____

Take a moment to sit in a circle, hold hands, and know that your love for one another will guide you to recovery from your grief.

# Letter to Your Loved One

Find a quiet, comfortable space to sit and write. You can all do this at the same time or at a time of your choice during the week. Allow yourself to write whatever comes to mind, knowing that there is no right or wrong way to do this. This is a private letter from you to your loved one, and it will not be judged by anyone.

Younger children might prefer to draw pictures of themselves with their loved one instead of writing. Be sure to give each of them a large sheet of paper and plenty of colors to draw with. You might ask them if they would like to share their pictures afterward.

In your letter (or picture) you might include...

- How you felt when you first learned of their death

- Any unanswered questions you have about their death

- Anything you were not able to say before or need to say now

- Any unresolved issues in your relationship

- What your life has been like since the loss

- What you miss most about them

- Some of your favorite memories with them

- How you are keeping their memory alive in your life

- Things you have learned about yourself or your loved one

- What you appreciate about the relationship you had and will take with you throughout your life

Find a time to sit as a family and share how you each felt about writing this letter. You may read your letters aloud or keep them to yourselves. Each family member can make their own decision about what they would like to do with the letter. Someone might seal it in an envelope and put it in a drawer. Another might want to leave it at the gravesite, let it go in a balloon, share it in a grief group, or create their own ritual with it.

# Creating a Loss Ritual

Rituals are actions that symbolize a person's feelings about the loved one and the painful loss they have experienced. They are a beautiful way to release emotions and maintain a connection to the loved one. They are also an important part of the mourning process that will help family members move through the grief process and toward peace and acceptance.

Family members can participate in these rituals on a daily, weekly, monthly, or annual basis, and creating them together can help family members feel connected and emotionally safe.

Here are some examples of rituals:

- Have a special weekly dinner in honor of the loved one, with each family member sharing a special thought or memory.

- Do something as a family that the loved one enjoyed.

- Light a candle at specific times, and share a thought aloud or silently about the loved one.

- Create a memory scrapbook.

- Listen to your loved one's favorite music, or watch a favorite movie.

- Plant a tree or flowers in honor of your loved one.

- Keep something special on you that reminds you of your loved one.

- Keep a daily journal of thoughts and feelings.

# 11

# Separation, Divorce, and Blended Families

## Therapist Preparation

Separation and divorce are never seamless processes for a family. Regardless of how well parents handle this difficult time, it does jar a family system, and it results in some period of grief. Whether the children are young or adults, their lives as they knew them have changed, and new norms need to be established.

Dissolution of marriage does not mean dissolution of family. As clinicians, it is our job to guide families through this process in a healthy manner, attending to any of the numerous emotional challenges that present themselves along the way. Young children often blame themselves for their parents' problems, and this guilt may manifest as anxiety, acting-out behaviors, trouble with school, changes in sleep and appetite, nightmares, and other symptoms. Adult children may also experience anxiety or depression, have questions about how and why this happened, and feel unsure of their own identity as the family system transforms.

## Telling Children about a Separation or Divorce

The following guidelines can help parents discuss the issue of separation or divorce with children:

1. Present a unified front and avoid any blame.
2. Tell them the truth in a simple, honest, and age-appropriate manner.
3. Let them know that you love them and that they are not to blame.
4. Sit close to your children, and give them a hug or hold their hand.
5. Let them know what the plan is and that some things will change while others will not.
6. Reassure them that you will always remain a family.
7. Allow them to share their feelings, making sure to reflect what you hear them say and to validate their feelings.
8. Reassure them that they may say whatever they feel without getting in any trouble.
9. Let them know that they may ask questions whenever they want and that you are always there for them.
10. Be prepared for their confusion and misunderstanding, and be sure to be patient and reassuring.
11. Provide as much stability and routine as possible while also maintaining rules and discipline.

## The Impact of Separation and Divorce on the Family System

1. There is an increase in disagreements and tension, as well as decreased family connection.
2. Family members experience anxiety as talk of separation increases.
3. Once separation has occurred, children often experience anxiety about with whom and where they and their siblings will live, and they may struggle with conflicted loyalties.
4. Family may experience financial stress and lifestyle changes.
5. Parents and children may experience symptoms of trauma, anxiety, guilt, and depression once the separation has occurred.
6. If new relationships or remarriage occur, children and parents face challenges adapting to the blended family.
7. Children may experience anxiety about parental attention to a new love interest.
8. Children may begin to act out, schoolwork may suffer, and substance use may occur.
9. Unhealthy co-parenting may put children in the middle position.

## Long-Term Family Goals

1. Both parents remain involved in children's lives.
2. Children are supported in spending time with each parent.
3. Parents communicate directly with each other.
4. Parents do not criticize or belittle each other to the children.
5. Parents help the children grieve the divorce or separation.
6. Parents reassure children they are not to blame.
7. Parents provide stability through the divorce or separation and afterward.
8. Parents seek help for the children should they experience mood or behavioral issues.
9. Self-care and support are made a priority for all family members.
10. Should parents remarry, efforts are made to bond with stepchildren and to develop stepfamily culture and rituals.

On the following pages are two separation, divorce, and blended family assignments to give to your clients one week at a time. In session, explain the topic to them using the sample conversation I have provided as a guide, and then describe the assignments to them, answering any questions they may have. If necessary, help the family modify the assignments to make them developmentally appropriate and understandable for all family members. Then send them home with the following assignments over the next two sessions, and process what they learned about separation, divorce, and blended families, as well as their experience of sharing about the topic with one another, in each subsequent session.

## Therapist Assignment Summaries

**Assignment #1:** *Separation, Divorce, and Blended Family Conversation*

The questions in this conversation will help guide family members to express their feelings about the current family situation, as well as to ask any questions and express any needs they have. Feel free to adjust or add questions as seems fitting.

**Assignment #2:** *Activities for Healing and Bonding*

The purpose of this three-part assignment is to provide each family member an opportunity to express and explore their feelings. They will make a "Home Is Where the Heart Is" journal and a "Place to Put My Feelings" box, and they'll create art that represents their feelings, which they may choose to share with one another.

Once they have completed both of the separation, divorce, and blended family assignments, and you have processed each in session, review the following goals in order to solidify their new understanding of this important topic.

## Separation, Divorce, and Blended Family Assignments Wrap-Up

"Now that you have done both of the separation, divorce, and blended family assignments, and we have talked about them in session, we are going to review some of what you learned. Do you feel that you…"

1.  (Children) Can ask your parents any questions you have and feel supported?
2.  (Children) Are not to blame for your parents' problems or decision to separate or divorce?
3.  Have coping tools for your anxiety and can ask for help if you need it?
4.  (Children) Are able to have quality time with each of your parents?
5.  Have been able to take the time you need to adjust to this new normal and to any new people in the family?
6.  (Children) Will always be a family regardless of whether your parents are married or not?
7.  (Children) Can still focus on other things in your life, like school, friends, and sports?

## Sample Conversation

Separation and divorce are always an emotional process for a family. It's normal to have some feelings of grief, such as sadness, anger, and anxiety, and what's really important is to remember that whether or not your parents remain together as a couple, you will always be a family. And it's really crucial that you children know that you are not at all responsible for any of your parents' problems or their decision to separate or divorce. Though your parents' feelings for each other have changed, their feelings of love for you will never change.

And I also want you children to know that you can ask your parents any questions anytime you want, and I want you parents to make sure you are always available to answer questions or give a big hug. Your parents are going to make sure that you know where you will be living and when you will see each of them. They will deal with all the adult decisions, and you just need to be children.

# Questions to Explore with Family Members

1. Children, are you able to ask your parents any questions you have?

   _____

   _____

2. Children, do you ever feel caught in the middle of your parents' arguments?

   _____

   _____

3. Children, is there anything you really need from your parents right now to help you to feel less anxious?

   _____

   _____

4. Parents, are you being careful about not sharing any of your negative feelings with the children?

   _____

   _____

5. Parents, have you reassured the children that they are not at all responsible for the problems in your relationship or marriage?

   _____

   _____

6. Parents, what have you done to create a stable environment for the children?

   _____

   _____

7. Parents, are you making it a priority to spend one-on-one time with each of the children?

   _____

   _____

8. What sort of things have you been doing to bond with new family members?

_____

_____

9. Parents, is there anything you can share now to reassure the children that you will always be a family?

_____

_____

I'm going to send you home today with one of two separation, divorce, and blended family assignments that are going to benefit you in three ways:

1. First, it is going to give you the opportunity to talk together about the changes in your family and to feel connected and supported by one another.

2. Next, you are going to start your own journal where you can write or draw pictures of your feelings.

3. And finally, you are going to complete two projects as a family that will help your family bond through this experience.

*Remember that you all are allowed to have the feelings you have.*
*Be kind and loving to one another.*

# Separation, Divorce, and Blended Family Conversation

*Love with your whole heart, and never be sorry you did.*
—Tonya D. Floyd

Create a comforting environment where you can have a difficult but important conversation about separation, divorce, or blended families. Make sure everyone is comfortable, turn your phones off, light a candle, and take a moment to close your eyes, take a few deep breaths, and then be present. You may choose a family member to take some notes while you ask these questions to your children, or you may simply talk and listen.

1. Do you all feel that regardless of what is happening, we will always be a family?

_____

_____

_____

2. Are there any questions you have that you haven't felt comfortable asking?

_____

_____

_____

3. Do you feel you are getting enough comfort and support from us parents?

_____

_____

_____

4. Do you truly understand that you are absolutely not to blame for what happened to our relationship or marriage?

_____

_____

_____

5. Can you each tell us something that you need right now to help make this easier for you?

_____

_____

_____

6. Is this situation getting in the way of your life outside the family? At school? With friends? With other activities?

_____

_____

_____

7. Do you feel that either of us is putting you in the middle of any of this?

_____

_____

_____

8. Do you have any fears about life going forward?

_____

_____

_____

9. Do you believe that you will always have a home with each of us and that you will always be our number-one priority?

_____

_____

_____

# Activities for Healing and Bonding
## "Home Is Where the Heart Is" Journal

Use a journal to write down your thoughts and feelings whenever you spend time at each parent's home. It can be as simple as describing how your day was at school, or you can focus more on how you are feeling, using words or pictures to do this. Remember that this is your private journal, and it's a special item to take back and forth with you. If you would like to share what you have written with your parents or siblings, that's fine, but you can also keep it to yourself.

Parents, you should keep a journal to express your feelings through this experience as well. If your children approve, it can be nice to leave them a special note on a blank page in their journal so they can read it when you are not with them.

**Suggested Journal Prompts**

- Today I am feeling...

- My favorite part of my day was...

- A difficult part of my day was...

- I am proud of myself for...

- One thing I appreciate about my life is...

- I am grateful for...

# Activities for Healing and Bonding
## "A Place to Put My Feelings" Box

- Obtain a shoebox or any other small box for each family member.

- Sit together as a group and decorate your box with stickers, pictures, paint, or anything else you'd like.

- Take a few moments each day to write a note about anything that is on your mind—any worries, any sadness, or even anything you are happy about.

- Place your note in your box, and know that both you and your feelings are safe and sound.

# Activities for Healing and Bonding
## Paint My Feelings Project

- Obtain a large sheet of paper or poster board for each family member.

- Have an assortment of paint colors at the center of the table.

- Paint your feelings on the page. Don't think too much about what you do, but instead allow whatever comes up to land on the page, whether this involves abstract shapes or an actual picture.

- Share your painting with your family, and talk about what it means to you and how it felt to make it.

# 12

# Anxiety and Depression

## Therapist Preparation

Anxiety and depression in a family member can greatly affect the functioning of the family system as a whole. As clinicians, it's important that we assess for this as we explore what may be interfering with the health of the family system. Keep in mind that it may also be necessary to advise the affected family member to seek a medical evaluation or assessment for medication.

Depression impairs parenting in many ways. Although much of the research has focused on maternal depression, it is important to be aware of depression among fathers as well. Parental depression may result in trouble bonding with and comforting a baby, which can impair the attachment process. It may also result in a decrease in responsiveness, verbal and visual interaction, praise, and participation in activities with the children. Discipline and supervision are often inconsistent, and the parent may become more irritable, hostile, or even abusive, resulting in chronic stress in the children. Parental anxiety may also result in the above behaviors, as well as a heightened need for control, which may agitate family members and create friction and resentment.

Children or adolescents of a parent with depression may exhibit greater acting-out behaviors, display more negative affect, have trouble regulating their feelings, and struggle with self-blame. They may have lower self-esteem and academic performance as well. Given that these children are also at greater risk of early-onset depression, aggression, and substance use, we must keep an eye on that as well. It's vital that family members understand the symptoms of depression and anxiety and their potential impact on the family system.

## The Impact of Anxiety and Depression on the Family System

1. Excessive worry or sadness impacts normal functioning at home and elsewhere.
2. Other family members are affected and may alter their needs or activities.
3. The family member with anxiety may irritate others with controlling behavior.
4. The family member with depression may become isolated.
5. Children with depression may have difficulty with concentration and memory, negatively impacting school functioning.
6. The family member with depression may become fatigued and irritable due to difficulty with sleep.
7. Children may act out in response to a parent who emotionally unavailable as a result of their depression or anxiety.
8. Children may become anxious or depressed due to their parents' mood.

## Long-Term Family Goals

1. Family member with depression or anxiety is able to identify and challenge underlying thoughts and beliefs that trigger symptoms.
2. Family receives education on the symptoms of anxiety or depression, the impact of these symptoms on the family system, and how to support each family member.
3. The family member with depression reengages with family.
4. All family members focus on developing healthy self-esteem.
5. Parent with anxiety or depression participates in family activities and reconnects with children who are acting out.
6. All family members practice self-care.
7. All family members are able to share the impact of anxiety or depression on their lives.

On the following pages are three anxiety and depression family assignments to give to your clients one week at a time. In session, explain the topic to them using the sample conversation I have provided as a guide, and then describe the assignments to them, answering any questions they may have. If necessary, help the family modify the assignments to make them developmentally appropriate and understandable for all family members. Then send them home with the following assignments over the next three sessions, and process what they learned about anxiety and depression, as well as their experience of sharing about the topic with one another, in each subsequent session.

## Therapist Assignment Summaries

**Assignment #1:** *Anxiety and Depression Conversation*

The questions in this conversation will help guide family members to express their feelings about anxiety and depression, as well as to ask any questions and express any needs they have. Feel free to adjust or add questions as seems fitting.

**Assignment #2:** *What I Think + What I Feel = What I Do or Don't Do*

The purpose of this assignment is to explore the impact of automatic thoughts and feelings on behavior.

**Assignment #3:** *Our Family Past and Present*

The purpose of this assignment is to explore any family history of anxiety or depression.

Once they have completed all three of the anxiety and depression assignments, and you have processed each in session, review the following goals to solidify their new understanding of this important topic.

## Anxiety and Depression Assignments Wrap-Up

"Now that you have done all three of the anxiety and depression assignments, and we have talked about them in session, we are going to review some of what you learned. Do you feel that you..."

1. Understand the symptoms of anxiety and depression and how they can affect your family?
2. Are more aware of some of your automatic thoughts and feelings that result in your being anxious or depressed?
3. Know some healthy things you can do to prevent or manage anxiety and depression?
4. Are able to ask for help with your feelings if you need it?

5. Have learned about some of your family history of anxiety and depression?

6. (Children) Did not cause your parents feelings or behaviors and are not responsible for taking care of them?

7. (Parents) Are now aware of how anxiety and depression may affect your children's self-esteem, behavior, academic success, friendships, energy, and attitude?

8. Are able to talk about your feelings, share your concern for one another if you see these symptoms, offer support, and ask for help if you need it?

## Sample Conversation

Anxiety and depression can be difficult to cope with and can really affect your whole family. When a parent is depressed or anxious, they often withdraw, become irritable, and have trouble enjoying their time with the family. And when children are depressed or anxious, they might have trouble sleeping, eating, getting along with people, and concentrating at school, and they may even get angry and do things they might not normally do.

Here are some really important things to know about depression and anxiety:

- Depression is a disorder that affects how a person feels, thinks, and acts.
- People with depression or anxiety may be impatient, irritable, and sad. They may cry, get tired easily, worry a lot, and have less energy to play.
- When people are depressed, their brains work differently.
- Depression is not a weakness, and it can have different causes.
- If you have a parent with depression or anxiety, they may do or say things that make you feel sad or confused.
- Children do not cause anxiety or depression, nor are they responsible for taking care of their parent.
- People can and do get better with help.
- It's important to talk about your feelings, be active, have the support of friends, and practice self-care.

# Questions to Explore with Family Members

1. Have any of you experienced feelings of anxiety and/or depression before or noticed them in another family member?

   _____

   _____

2. Children, do you notice that your parents seem different sometimes?

   _____

   _____

3. Children, do you ever blame yourself if your parents are in a bad mood?

   _____

   _____

4. Parents, are you able to share some of your feelings with your children?

   _____

   _____

5. Parents, do you understand how anxiety or depression can affect your children's moods or behaviors?

   _____

   _____

6. Are there any things that you find are helpful to do when you are feeling sad or anxious?

   _____

   _____

I'm going to send you home today with one of three anxiety and depression assignments that are going to benefit you in three ways:

1. First, it is going to give you an opportunity to talk together about anxiety and depression and to feel connected and supported by one another.

2. Next, you are going to learn how to pay attention to your thoughts and feelings and to change your thoughts if you need to.

3. And finally, you are going to complete a family genogram, which will help you to discover any history of anxiety or depression in your family.

*Remember that you all are allowed to have the feelings you have.*
*Be kind and loving to one another.*

# Coping with Anxiety and Depression Family Conversation

*Once you choose hope, anything's possible.*
—Christopher Reeve

Create a comforting environment where you can have a difficult but important conversation about anxiety and depression. Make sure everyone is comfortable, turn your phones off, light a candle, and take a moment to close your eyes, take a few deep breaths, and then be present. You may choose a family member to take some notes or simply talk and listen.

1. Are you struggling with any of these symptoms of depression?

   • Tearfulness

   • Sadness

   • Lack of interest in activities

   • Fatigue

   • Trouble sleeping

   • Appetite changes

   • Feelings of guilt

   • Feelings of hopelessness

   • Thoughts of self-harm

If so, which ones?

_____

_____

_____

2. Are you struggling with any of these symptoms of anxiety?

- Restlessness

- Irritability

- Fatigue

- Sweating

- Worry

- Nausea

- A sense of impending doom or that something terrible is going to happen

- Fear of something specific (e.g., an animal, a location, an activity)

- Fear of social situations

- Feeling you are going crazy or having a heart attack

If so, which ones are they?

_____

_____

_____

3. Are you comfortable talking to us about these feelings?

_____

_____

_____

4. Is there anything in particular that makes you feel anxious or depressed?

_____

_____

_____

5. Is there anything we can do to help you with these feelings?

_____

_____

_____

6. Do you know that it's normal to have feelings of anxiety or depression at times in life?

_____

_____

_____

7. What is one nice thing you can say to each family member right now?

_____

_____

_____

8. What is something you like about yourself?

_____

_____

_____

9. What is one thing you do to help yourself when you feel anxious?

_____

_____

_____

10. Are you worried about anyone in our family struggling with anxiety or depression?

_____

_____

_____

11. Do you believe that you are responsible for any family member's anxiety or depression?

_____

_____

_____

# What I Think + How I Feel = What I Do or Don't Do

Your thoughts are incredibly powerful. You might be surprised to know how automatically you have a thought after something happens and how quickly a feeling then occurs, which finally leads to a decision to behave one way or another.

**For instance:**

- *What happened:* I didn't do well on my math quiz.

- *What I thought:* "I'm such a loser. Everyone else is smarter. Why bother studying?"

- *What I felt:* Sad, discouraged

- *What I did:* Didn't talk to my friends at lunch. Watched TV at home and didn't do my homework. Was grumpy toward my parents.

Now, what if my first thought had been positive?

- *New thought:* "I'm disappointed about my grade on the quiz, but I know that I tried hard. I'm sure I'll do better the next time, and I bet I wasn't the only one who didn't do well."

- *What I might feel instead:* Disappointed but not discouraged

- *What might I do instead:* Enjoy my friends at lunch, go home and tell my parents, and then do my homework and enjoy my evening.

Noticing your automatic negative thoughts allows you to quickly adjust them to be more positive and accurate, which is more likely to help you feel better and to do things that will be kinder to yourself.

Now, think of a time when something happened that upset you, and answer the following questions:

I remember a time when...

_____

_____

_____


My thoughts when that happened were...

_____

_____

_____

The feelings I had then were...

_____

_____

_____

What I did or didn't do after that was...

_____

_____

**If that were to happen to me again:**

I would like to think these positive thoughts...

_____

_____

_____

I would then most likely feel...

_____

_____

_____

With those more positive thoughts and feelings, I would probably do or not do...

_____

_____

_____

Take turns sharing your responses with one another, and then talk about what you have learned about your automatic thoughts and how you will try to be kinder to yourself going forward.

# Our Family Past and Present

Just as you inherit physical traits from your family and ancestors, you can inherit emotional traits as well. Some of these are genetic traits, and some are a result of family behaviors that are passed down across generations. Exploring your family history can help you understand why you are the way you are and allow you to think about what traits you may be able to change with some awareness and effort.

Below is a **genogram**, which is a type of family tree used to explore the various personality, behavioral, and emotional traits of family members, both past and present.

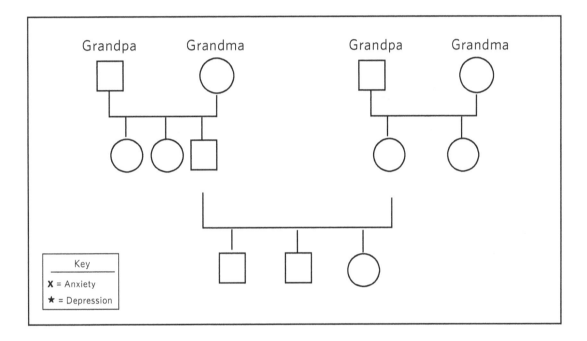

Using a red pen, make note of any family members that have struggled with *anxiety*, and using a blue pen, make note of any that have struggled with *depression*. Feel free to go back as many generations as you can and to add any other family members or personality traits.

Next, have a conversation about any patterns of anxiety, depression, and personality traits that you notice.

# 13

# Eating Disorders

## Therapist Preparation

Eating disorders can affect anyone, at any age, and of any gender, socioeconomic status, sexual orientation, race, or ethnicity. According to the National Association of Anorexia Nervosa and Associated Disorders, over 30 million Americans experience an eating disorder during their lifetime, with an estimated 30–50 percent of these individuals suffering from a comorbid mood disorder. In addition, anorexia has the highest rate of mortality of any mental illness.

If a family member is suffering from an eating disorder, the whole family is affected. They often want so much to help and yet feel powerless when change does not happen, which can lead to anger, resentment, anxiety, and denial.

Recovery from an eating disorder is possible, and early detection greatly increases the potential for success. Unfortunately, only approximately 30 percent of people do seek treatment. Therefore, when we are treating a family member with a mood disorder, it is important that we be on the lookout for any potential symptoms of a comorbid eating disorder.

## Some Warning Signs and Symptoms

- Preoccupation with weight, food, calories, exercise, and dieting
- Discomfort eating around others
- Rituals around food
- Skipping meals and eating small portions
- Withdrawal from friends and activities
- Mood swings
- Weight fluctuations
- Nonspecific gastrointestinal issues
- Dizziness, fainting, feeling cold, difficulty with sleep, weakness, and trouble concentrating
- Dry skin and hair, brittle nails, cavities, and calloused fingers due to induced vomiting

If you do diagnose a family member with an eating disorder, you must then determine in which stage of recovery they are in order to guide your treatment plan.

## Stages of Recovery

*Pre-contemplation Stage:*

- Affected family member does not believe they have a problem.
- If the affected member is a child, parents must not be in denial, must be aware of signs and symptoms, and must share concerns.
- Psychotherapist educates family about symptoms and makes referrals as necessary.

*Contemplation Stage:*

- Affected family member is willing to admit they have a problem and is open to receiving help.
- Family members must not attempt to treat the problem themselves but must instead insist on professional help if the affected family member is a minor or encourage and facilitate professional help if they are older than 18.
- Psychotherapist can now help identify the role that the eating disorder has played in the client's life and how it no longer serves them and can then guide them toward healthy change.

*Preparation Stage:*

- Affected family member is helped by a treatment team consisting of a psychotherapist, nutritionist, and physician.
- Parents learn their role in supporting the family member's recovery and beliefs regarding food and weight.
- Psychotherapist focuses on developing coping skills, creating boundaries, practicing assertiveness, and challenging eating-disordered thinking with cognitive behavioral therapy (CBT).

*Action Stage:*

- Affected family member trusts the treatment team, faces their fears, and implements new behaviors.
- Parents are warm, supportive, and make adjustments as per the treatment team.
- Psychotherapist processes feelings as the family moves through recovery.

*Maintenance/Relapse Stage:*

- Affected family member has maintained healthy recovery for six months and has established coping mechanisms for potential triggers.
- Parents continue to emotionally support and validate the family member's efforts and successes.
- Psychotherapist continues to help family members practice any new boundaries and communication skills and educates the family about potential signs of relapse.

## The Impact of Eating Disorders on the Family System

1. The family system is characterized by anxiety due to the affected member's denial of weight loss, eating habits, and disordered behavior (e.g., bingeing, purging, restricting).
2. The affected member becomes defensive when confronted by others, causing tension in the family.
3. The affected member disconnects from the family.
4. Parental focus is on the affected family member and less on other children.
5. Anger and resentment may develop in other family members.

## Long-Term Family Goals

1.  Family becomes educated about eating disorders and develops an understanding that this condition is not a choice, that there is not one specific cause, and that the affected family member is not emotionally well.

2.  Affected family member seeks treatment and establishes normal eating patterns. Physical and emotional health improves, and this improvement continues with support systems in place.

3.  Family members are able to express and process the impact of the eating disorder on their life.

4.  Family patterns and beliefs influencing the affected member, as well as other family members, are addressed and corrected.

5.  Family is restored to a state of emotional stability and connection.

6.  Family is aware of warning signs and symptoms of relapse, and they have an action plan in place.

On the following pages are three eating disorder family assignments to give to your clients one week at a time. In session, explain the topic to them using the sample conversation I have provided as a guide, and then describe the assignments to them, answering any questions they may have. If necessary, help the family modify the assignments to make them developmentally appropriate and understandable for all family members. Then send them home with the following assignments over the next three sessions, and process what they learned about eating disorders, as well as their experience of sharing about the topic with one another, in each subsequent session.

## Therapist Assignment Summaries

**Assignment #1:** *Eating Disorder Family Conversation*

The questions in this conversation will help guide family members to express their feelings about the current family situation, as well as to ask any questions and express any needs they have. Feel free to adjust or add questions as seems fitting.

**Assignment #2:** *Myths and Truths about Eating Disorders Quiz*

The purpose of this assignment is to educate family members about eating disorders. Prior to giving them this assignment, cut and fold each of the fifteen questions, and put them in individual envelopes that the family can open one by one when they do the assignment.

**Assignment #3:** *A Letter to Your Loved One*

The purpose of this assignment is to have each family member write a guided letter to their loved one to show support and share feelings. They will share this letter aloud at home and should then do the same in the next session and process with you.

Once they have completed all three of the eating disorder assignments, and they have processed each in session with you, review the following goals to solidify their new understanding of this important topic.

## Eating Disorder Assignments Wrap-Up

"Now that you have completed all three of the eating disorder assignments, and we have talked about them in session, we are going to review some of what you learned. Do you feel that you..."

1. Can define what an eating disorder is and is not?

2. Are aware of any family patterns that might have contributed to you or your loved one having an eating disorder?

3. (Affected family member) Are able to share more openly about any feelings or situations that might trigger your eating disorder and that you can ask for help?

4. (Affected family member) Are aware of any automatic thoughts, feelings, behaviors, or assumptions that may affect healthy eating for you?

5. Understand the importance of healthy boundaries, assertiveness, communication, acceptance, and conflict resolution in having positive family dynamics?

6. Understand how extremely important it is to be loved and valued for your own personality, temperament, likes, and dislikes, and to avoid judgment and criticism of yourself and one another?

## Sample Conversation

As I'm sure you know, when one family member has an eating disorder, it affects the whole family. I'm sure there have been times when you have tried to help your loved one, but they have become angry, sad, or resentful. It's really hard to see someone you love suffer and to worry about what will happen if they don't realize they have a problem and seek help.

It's also really important that you all have a chance to talk about how you feel and to have support and help. Your mental, emotional, and physical health is so important, and you can only help one another when you also help yourself. I'm here to help you all understand what an eating disorder really is and what the stages of recovery are for your loved one.

There are different kinds of eating disorders, but generally speaking, an eating disorder involves an extreme concern about body size and shape, which affects that person's eating behaviors. There are a number of different ways this may occur. For instance, they may restrict their eating, or they may overeat and then purge or exercise in an extreme way, or they may periodically binge eat.

It's important to know that eating disorders don't just have one cause, nor is anyone to blame, nor should anyone feel any shame for struggling with this problem. No one chooses to have an eating disorder. These conditions are biopsychosocial disorders, which means they are affected by biological, emotional, and socio-environmental factors. Fortunately, they can be treated, and your loved one can recover and live a healthy life.

There are five stages of recovery, and we are going to begin where you are and work together from there. The stages are pre-contemplation, contemplation, preparation, action, and maintenance. (Identify what stage the family member with the eating disorder is in and what that means for their recovery process.)

# Questions to Explore
# with Family Members

1. How has your loved one's eating disorder affected you?

   _____

   _____

2. Do you feel some relief that you can work together as a family to support your loved one through recovery?

   _____

   _____

3. Do you understand that no one is to blame, that there is no single cause, and that your loved one cannot control this, nor are they doing it for attention?

   _____

   _____

4. (Affected family member) How are you feeling now that we are going to work together to help you become healthy again?

   _____

   _____

5. Do you have any questions for me about what comes next?

   _____

   _____

6. Is there anything you need from your family to help you through this?

   _____

   _____

I'm going to send you home today with one of three eating disorder assignments that are going to benefit you in three ways:

1. First, you are going to have an opportunity to talk together about eating disorders and to feel connected and supported by one another.

2. Next, you are going to learn some of the myths about eating disorders so you can have a better understanding of what they are and truly help your loved one.

3. And finally, you are going to write a letter to your loved one that expresses your support and feelings, and then share as a family.

*Remember that you all are allowed to have the feelings you have.*
*Be kind and loving to one another.*

# Eating Disorder Conversation

*You, yourself, as much as anybody in the entire universe,
deep breaths deserve your love and affection.*

—Buddha

Create a comforting environment where you can have a difficult but important conversation about eating disorders. Make sure everyone is comfortable, turn your phones off, light a candle, and take a moment to close your eyes, take a few deep breaths, and then be present. You may choose a family member to take some notes, or simply talk and listen.

1. Do we all understand that an eating disorder is not a choice, that no one is to blame, and that [*name of family member with eating disorder*] should not feel any shame for struggling with this?

   _____

   _____

   _____

2. Do you see this as an opportunity for us to grow together as a family?

   _____

   _____

   _____

3. Children, do you feel that we parents put too much pressure on you to be perfect or successful?

   _____

   _____

   _____

4. Do any of you feel criticized or judged by anyone in the family?

   _____

   _____

   _____

5. (Affected family member) Can you share with us what any of the triggers are for your eating disorder and how we might help you?

   _____

   _____

   _____

# Myths and Truths about Eating Disorders

First, have each person get a piece of paper and write "True" on one side of the paper and "False" on the other side. Then take turns reading each statement. After each statement, determine if it is true or false by holding up the "True" or "False" side of your paper. Finally, read the answers that follow this exercise, and talk about what you have learned with your family.

**Statement #1:**

Eating disorders are a choice, and my loved one should just stop.

**Statement #2:**

Our loved one's eating disorder was caused by the parenting style in our family.

**Statement #3:**

There are several types of harmful eating disorders.

**Statement #4:**

Parental involvement is very important in recovering from an eating disorder.

**Statement #5:**

If my loved one seems fine, then I don't need to be concerned about them.

**Statement #6:**

My loved one can recover from the eating disorder even if they don't discover a specific reason for their eating disorder.

**Statement #7:**

Eating disorders aren't always a problem.

**Statement #8:**

People with eating disorders don't always look emaciated.

**Statement #9:**

If someone appears to be a normal weight, they probably don't have an eating disorder.

**Statement #10:**

People with eating disorders may also obsess about things like grades, sports performance, and looking perfect.

**Statement #11:**

Only girls suffer from eating disorders.

**Statement #12:**

Children as young as age five can suffer from eating disorders.

**Statement #13:**

Everyone binges on food sometimes.

**Statement #14:**

Purging can involve more than vomiting.

**Statement #15:**

Once someone with anorexia gains weight, they will be fine.

Answer #1: **False**

An eating disorder is a complex medical and psychological illness and not something that one chooses. There are often genetic, family-system, and psychological factors involved. A person suffering from an eating disorder should never be shamed or accused of choosing to suffer from an eating disorder.

Answer #2: **False**

Although a family culture of perfectionism and rigid expectations may contribute, the American Psychiatric Association guidelines indicate that parents do not cause an eating disorder in a child. There is no set formula for parenting that will prevent an eating disorder, but it is generally thought that a nonjudgmental, accepting environment that encourages self-acceptance and self-esteem will help a loved one in recovery from an eating disorder.

Answer #3: **True**

The most common eating disorders are:

- *Anorexia nervosa:* An obsessive fear of weight gain, a refusal to maintain a healthy weight, and a distorted body image.

- *Bulimia nervosa:* Repeated episodes of binge-eating (eating large amounts of food in short periods of time) and purging (eliminating the calories consumed) at least once a week for three months.

- *Binge-eating disorder:* Recurrent episodes of rapid overeating, even when not hungry, often then feeling extremely full, and feeling out of control while doing this.

Answer #4: **True**

Research does find that parental involvement in recovery from eating disorders is very important. Parental support, love, and encouragement can help to reduce anxiety and increase hopefulness in a loved one's recovery.

Answer #5: **False**

A loved one with an eating disorder may not be aware of how unhealthy they are and may insist they do not have a problem, or they may not admit to their struggle due to fear of treatment. It is important to follow through with treatment for your loved one if they have been diagnosed with an eating disorder.

Answer #6: **True**

There is no evidence that it is necessary to identify a specific cause of an eating disorder in order to recover. The main goal of treatment is to restore healthy eating and weight through cognitive and behavioral changes.

Answer #7: **False**

Eating disorders severely impact an individual's quality of life, and if left untreated, they may even result in death. It is always important to take them seriously and seek professional help.

Answer #8: **True**

It is not possible to determine if someone has an eating disorder just by looking at them. Although they may have returned to a healthy weight, they may still be struggling with disordered thinking.

Answer #9: **False**

Restrictive eating disorders, such as anorexia nervosa, do involve weight loss, yet some people with eating disorders actually gain weight due to bingeing, and others maintain a normal weight due to bingeing and purging.

Answer #10: **True**

Loved ones struggling with eating disorders may obsess about things other than food, such as getting good grades, winning at sports, and looking perfect. It's important for parents to focus on a family culture of validation, acceptance, and nonjudgment versus the goal of perfection and excellence.

Answer #11: **False**

There have been a growing number of boys and men with eating disorders. It is uncertain whether this is because the disorder has increased in males or because they have begun to report symptoms more openly and often. Therefore, it is important to be aware of the disorder in young boys and men as well.

Answer #12: **True**

Children as young as age five may struggle with eating disorders. Adolescents and adults with eating disorders have also reported that the onset of their disordered thinking about food and weight began at a very young age. It is important for parents to validate children for who they are and what they do as opposed to how they look.

Answer #13: **False**

Many of us may eat more than we feel comfortable with from time to time. Binge eating is different in that it involves a lack of control while eating more food in a shorter period of time than most people would, and this becomes a recurring pattern.

Answer #14: **True**

While many people assume that a loved one with an eating disorder will purge by vomiting, it's important to be aware of other methods, such as laxatives, enemas, fasting, and excessive exercising. It is also possible that they will vary their methods of purging.

Answer #15: **False**

Once a loved one returns to a healthy weight and develops a habit of healthy nutrition, it is essential that they continue to focus on emotional health and maintain a healthy support system. Parents can help with this by participating in family therapy, practicing healthy communication with their children, and making family connection a priority.

# A Letter to Your Loved One

Each of you will write a letter to your loved one using the following template to help. Share your feelings openly while remembering to be respectful and loving. When you are all ready, sit together in a comfortable and calm place and take turns reading aloud your letters to your loved one.

[*Loved one's name*] _____, I want to begin this letter by telling

you how much I love you. You are such an important person in my life, and I have so many

memories with you. Some of my best memories are _____

_____

_____.

I really respect you for _____

_____,

and I think the most beautiful thing about you is _____

_____

_____.

I know that you are really struggling with your eating disorder, and it makes me feel

_____ that you are going through this.

I worry about _____

_____.

and I really hope that _____

_____.

I am going to support you by _____

_____.

and I also want you to let me know if there are any other ways that I can support you and make this time a little easier for you.

[*Loved one's name*] _____, you are always going to be

my [*sister, brother, son, daughter*] _____,

and we have so much to look forward to. I'm excited to share more wonderful times with

you doing things like _____

_____

_____.

You have so many strengths, and my dream for your future is _____

_____

_____.

I know that your recovery will be a lifelong journey, and I want you to know that you are not alone as we will walk this path together forever.

I love you,

_____

# 14

# Adoption and Fostering

## Therapist Preparation

Couples and individuals adopt or foster children for many reasons. It may be due to infertility, a wish to expand a family, a desire to offer a warm and loving home to a child in need, a kinship adoption as a result of the death of a family member, or a variety of other reasons, such as being in a same-sex partnership. Children may be adopted from the United States or other countries, may range from newborn age to adolescents younger than 18, and may not be of the same race as the family they join. And in the case of foster children, they may join a family individually or as part of a group.

The decision to adopt involves a great deal of thought, patience, preparation, and emotion, and it can create tension in a couple when both may not be on the same page with the decision. There is also often a great deal of anxiety and fear, and for those who have struggled with infertility, there is generally a prior process of grieving the inability to have a biological child. For individuals or couples who already have children, there is also a delicate process of blending biological and adoptive children and creating an environment where everyone feels equally loved, valued, and cared for.

Fostering a child has some unique concerns as well. Many children in the foster system have special needs and may have experienced substantial abuse, neglect, trauma, and attachment injury. It is important for these parents to be aware of the many services available to assist with financial, emotional, medical, or academic challenges.

As psychotherapists, it is our job to support potential adoptive and foster parents through the decision process, to normalize the many emotions and challenges they may have once the process is complete, and to educate and continue providing support throughout the numerous stages and adjustments they will experience going forward.

Adoption experts Sharon Kaplan Roszia and Allison Davis Maxon have identified seven core issues in adoption and permanency, which are listed below, along with possible manifestations that may arise if these issues are not managed in a healthy manner with support from parents and family:

1. **Loss:** The event that resulted in the need to adopt or foster may result in loss of family culture and history and a sense of powerlessness in life going forward.
2. **Rejection:** Underlying sense of abandonment, which may manifest as sensitivity to any perceived rejection going forward, as well as self-blame.
3. **Shame and Guilt:** Feelings of being bad and undeserving, which may manifest as a loud inner critic and result in their entering into abusive or neglectful future relationships.
4. **Grief:** The result of the original loss and any feelings of rejection, shame, and guilt. This may occur with the initial separation or when a child learns of their adoption and becomes triggered again when others ask questions.

5. **Identity:** Throughout life, children may have identity issues related to adoption, which may manifest as anger, sadness, or a desire to have contact with their biological parents.

6. **Intimacy:** A desire to feel that they belong, are valued, and know what they need in a relationship. This may manifest as difficulty with intimacy and authenticity.

7. **Mastery and Control:** A desire to feel secure and in control in life. This may manifest as insecurity, anxiety, or emotional disconnect.

In order to help children successfully navigate these core issues, the following parental traits are advised:

1. Live in the present and validate small successes.

2. Understand that there may be moments of rejection from the child, and maintain consistent, unconditional love and acceptance.

3. Have self-compassion when experiencing moments of frustration or negative feelings with the child.

4. Each parent must be sensitive to times when the other needs a break and be happy to relieve them. In the case of single parents, they must give themselves permission to ask for help and build a network of support.

5. Transition quickly from new parent to solidified parent, setting boundaries, expectations, and consequences, while nurturing and developing emotional attachment and intimacy. See the family as a system and the child as a unique individual with their own identity.

6. Understand that a successful transition requires a conscious effort to connect with the adoptive or foster child. Offer praise, affection, and positive reinforcement, while also communicating and following through with rules and consequences.

7. Value and model self-care, with the recognition that doing so will allow parents to feel refreshed.

8. Be able to use humor and be playful.

9. Be vulnerable and ask for help and education from available support systems.

## Communicating with Your Adopted Child

1. Make *adoption* a household word from the beginning.

2. Practice how to have a conversation about how your family became a family many times before you actually do so. That way, it is a comfortable story when you share it with your child when they are ready.

3. Talk about birth parents in a proud manner so your child doesn't interpret them as bad people from whom they might have inherited bad characteristics.

4. If you are unprepared to answer a question, let the child know that it is a good question and that you need just a little time (no more than a couple of days) to give them a good answer.

5. Make the conversation age-appropriate.

6. Be open and honest.

7. Share gratitude and excitement about having them in your life.

8. Be aware that this will be an ongoing conversation.

# The Impact of Adoption or Fostering on the Family System

1. Parents may experience grief due to previous struggles with infertility.
2. There may be tension in the family relationship when deciding whether to adopt or foster.
3. In an open adoption, the relationship between the biological and adoptive parents will evolve over time.
4. The child may have suffered trauma, abuse, or neglect.
5. The child may suffer symptoms of grief due to the loss of their birth family.
6. The child may experience shame or guilt if taken away from their birth family.
7. The child may fear further rejection, abandonment, or loss.
8. The child may experience identity challenges.
9. Challenges with attachment may occur, often related to the age of adoption.
10. Foster or adoptive teenagers may test boundaries and have chronic behavioral issues.
11. Biological and adoptive children may have challenges bonding and finding their place in the family.

# Long-Term Family Goals

1. If parents have experienced infertility, they are able to process and resolve any feelings of grief or shame.
2. Parents successfully work through the decision-making process to adopt or foster.
3. If there are biological children, they are lovingly informed about the decision to adopt or foster, their questions are answered, and they are given ongoing reassurance about their place in the family and the unchanging love and support from their parents.
4. Parents and the adoptive or foster child form a healthy, secure bond.
5. Parents make use of the many support systems available.
6. Biological and adoptive children resolve any tension and bond with one another.
7. Parents disclose child's adoption history in an age-appropriate manner.

On the following pages are three adoption and fostering assignments to give to your clients one week at a time. In session, explain the topic to them using the sample conversation I have provided as a guide, and then describe the assignments to them, answering any questions they may have. If necessary, help the family modify the assignments to make them developmentally appropriate and understandable for all family members. Then send them home with the following assignments over the next three sessions, and process what they learned about adoption and fostering, as well as their experience of sharing about the topic with one another, in each subsequent session.

# Therapist Assignment Summaries

**Assignment #1:** *Adoption and Fostering Family Conversation*

The questions in this conversation will help guide family members to express their feelings about the current family situation, as well as to ask any questions and express any needs they may have. Feel free to adjust or add questions as seems fitting.

**Assignment #2:** *Blending Biological and Adoptive/Foster Children*

The purpose of this assignment is to offer three opportunities for the biological children and parents to connect with the adopted or foster child. The first activity is a conversation between the parents and the biological children about the upcoming adoption. The second activity is a family journal that will help strengthen the family bond by allowing members to share feelings about a new topic each week. The third activity is a letter that the parents and biological children will write to the new family member.

**Assignment #3:** *Our Family Collage*

The purpose of this assignment is for the family to bond with a fun activity that also helps them to see themselves as a cohesive, connected family.

Once they have completed all three of the adoption and fostering assignments, and you have processed each in session, review the following goals to solidify their new understanding of this important topic.

## Adoption and Fostering Assignments Wrap-Up

"Now that you have completed all three of the adoption and fostering assignments, and we have talked about them in session, we are going to review some of what you learned. Do you feel that you…"

1. Have worked through your decision-making process and are in agreement?
2. (If applicable) Have worked through the pain and grief of your infertility struggles?
3. Understand some of the potential challenges of adopting or fostering a child?
4. Understand how important it will be to reach out to the support systems available to you and your child?
5. Know the parenting traits that will help your adoptive or foster child to acclimate to your home and family and allow the bonding process to be successful between the parents and the child?
6. Understand that there may be moments of rejection by your adoptive or foster child?
7. Understand the seven core issues that adoptive and foster children often experience, including how important it is to support them through these issues so they may have a healthy outcome?
8. Understand how to share your decision to adopt or foster a child with your biological children so they feel secure in your love and their position in the family?

## Sample Conversation

The most basic definition of family is "a group consisting of parents and children living together in a household"—which you certainly all are. How a family looks and how parents and children come together may vary, but the result is the same. You become a tribe, a team, a squad, however you describe it, but the bottom line is that you are a group of people who love, care about, and support one another. You share a home, share your dreams, and even if you don't always agree or get along, in the end you know that these are your people and that whatever happens, your parents will take care of you and keep you safe.

Being a family with adoptive or foster kids makes you unique and special, and over the next few weeks we are going to talk about your experience in this great family. Whether you became a part of a family at birth, as a baby, as a toddler, or as an adolescent, your experience is all your own, and we want to know all about it … happy things and sad things too.

# Questions to Explore
# with Family Members

1. What are your earliest memories of becoming a part of your family?

   _____

   _____

2. Are there any questions you have wanted to ask but haven't?

   _____

   _____

3. What do you love most about your family?

   _____

   _____

4. Is there anything that makes you sad or angry about being a part of your family?

   _____

   _____

5. (Adoptive or foster child) Has being an adoptive or foster child affected your life outside of your family in any way?

   _____

   _____

6. Is there anything you would want to change about your life?

   _____

   _____

7. Parents, how has your experience of adopting or fostering a child changed your life?

   _____

   _____

8. (Biological child) How has having an adoptive or foster sibling felt for you?

_____

_____

I'm going to send you home today with one of three adoption and fostering assignments that are going to benefit you in three ways:

1. First, you are going to have an opportunity to talk together about the beauty of expanding your family with adoptive and foster children so you all feel more bonded and loved.

2. Next, parents, you will have a conversation with your biological child about having an adoptive or foster child become a part of your family. You will then all create a new family journal and write a loving letter to your new family member.

3. And finally, together you are going to create a collage that represents your wonderful family.

*Remember that you all are allowed to have the feelings you have.*
*Be kind and loving to one another.*

# Adoption and Fostering
# Family Conversation

*Give me the place to stand, and I will move the earth.*
—Archimedes

Create a comforting environment where you can have a loving conversation about being a family. Make sure everyone is comfortable, turn your phones off, light a candle, and take a moment to close your eyes, take a few deep breaths, and then be present. You may choose a family member to take some notes or simply talk and listen.

1. What made us parents decide that we wanted to adopt or foster a child?

_____

_____

_____

2. How did we feel when we first met you and welcomed you to your new home?

_____

_____

_____

3. What are each of our first memories of living here together?

_____

_____

_____

4. (Adoptive or foster child) How did you feel when you learned that we had adopted or fostered you?

_____

_____

_____

5. What does family mean to you?

_____

_____

_____

6. (Adoptive or foster child) Are there times when you feel angry or sad about being an adoptive or foster child of ours?

_____

_____

_____

7. (Adoptive or foster child) Do you feel that we are loving and supportive of you when you are having those difficult feelings?

_____

_____

_____

8. (Biological child) How did you feel when we told you we were going to adopt or foster a child or when you were old enough to understand that?

_____

_____

_____

9. What does it mean to you to be a sibling?

_____

_____

_____

10. (Adoptive or foster child) Do you feel like it's okay to ask questions about your biological parents?

_____

_____

_____

11. (Adoptive or foster child) Do you believe that the love of a parent has nothing to do with who gave birth to you?

_____

_____

_____

# Blending Biological and Adoptive/Foster Children

## A Conversation with Your Biological Child

Before an adoptive or foster child becomes a member of your family, have a conversation with your biological children using the following prompts:

- [*Adoptive or foster child's name*]'s parents placed them up for adoption because

  _____.

- Their biological parent searched for the perfect family, and when they met us, they knew that we were the family that [*adoptive or foster child's name*] was meant to be with.

- We all need to feel loved, just like we love you, and we have enough love and attention for all of us. [*Adoptive or foster child's name*] may feel sad or scared when they first come here, so we are going to help them feel loved too. Do you have any ideas about how we can do that?

- And I really want you to help us prepare for them to live here, so will you help me get some things for them? What do you think they might need?

Now, let's draw a picture of how our family will look with [*adopted/foster child's name*] here:

**147**

# Blending Biological and Adoptive/Foster Children

## Family Journal

Begin a journal that you will work on together as a family once a week. Each week, a different family member will write a prompt for a conversation, and afterward, each family member will draw a picture or write a few sentences about what they would like share. You may also record responses on video as a lovely way to revisit the conversations.

---

**Example:**

### OUR FAMILY JOURNAL

**Date:** April 26th          **Family leader:** Mom

**Prompt:** What was your favorite moment this week?

| Name | Response |
|------|----------|
| Annie | My favorite moment was when we all took the dog to the park together. It was fun to laugh and play as a family, and I can't wait to do it again. |
| Jack | I liked sleeping in five extra minutes before school. |

---

**Date:**                    **Family leader:**

| Name | Response |
|------|----------|
|  |  |
|  |  |
|  |  |
|  |  |
|  |  |

---

# Blending Biological and Adoptive/Foster Children

## A Letter to My New Loved One

Write a letter to your new family member. Use the following points to help guide you. When you are all done, share the letters aloud. Encourage your adoptive or foster child to share their feelings about the letters and about being a new member of the family.

**Possible topics:**

- How you felt when you first learned you were going to have a new sibling or child

- Any questions or concerns you had

- How your sibling or child has enriched your life and family

- What you have learned about your sibling or child

- Any challenges you have overcome as you bonded together

- Any similarities you have learned about one another

- Things you enjoy doing together

- Things you look forward to doing together

- How you hope your sibling or child felt about becoming part of your family

- What you love about your sibling or child

- What your dream is for your sibling or child

- What you might like to thank your sibling or child for

**Younger children may find these prompts helpful:**

[*Adoptive or foster child's name*], I am really happy to have you as my sibling because

_____

_____.

I have fun with you when we _____

_____.

You are special to me because _____

_____.

When you first became my sibling, I didn't know you well, but I now know that your favorite

food is _____, your favorite color is _____,

and your favorite hobby, toy, or sport is _____.

I look forward to doing or sharing these things with you: _____

_____.

I want you to know that I love you because _____

_____.

I want to thank you for _____

_____.

# Our Family Collage

**Materials:**

- Large piece of poster board for each family member

- Magazines

- Scissors

- Glue

Sit together around a table and chat as you each tear or cut out magazines pictures that represent you and your family.

Next, glue these pictures onto the poster board, look at your masterpiece as a group, and then talk about how your family and life together looks in pictures.

**Here are a few conversation prompts:**

How do you feel when you look at the collage?

_____

_____

What is your favorite part of the collage?

_____

_____

Do any memories pop up when you look at the collage?

_____

_____

What do you see in the collage that is unique to your family?

_____

_____

If you were to give the collage a title, what would it be?

_____

_____

# 15

# Verbal, Emotional, and Physical Domestic Abuse

## Therapist Preparation

Although other species can be aggressive, only humans are capable of abuse. That is because, as humans, we are capable of understanding how others *should* be treated. And although the triggers for abusive behavior are generally unconscious, the decision to engage in abusive behavior is still a conscious one. Abusers are able to control their behavior. They are able to maintain their composure around bosses, neighbors, and anyone else whose opinion of them matters. Therefore, in the moment before they act out, there is a choice that is made to proceed with an abusive word or action.

Domestic abuse involves a pattern of intimidation, as well as physical and/or emotional assault, that occurs in the context of intimate relationships. The intention is to maintain power and control over the victimized partner. Abusers are often charismatic and manipulative. As a result, outsiders may find it difficult to believe someone when they share what they are experiencing at home, which may then make the victim second-guess their feelings.

Abuse is cyclical. Abusers may go long periods of time acting regretful, behaving caringly, and maintaining the status quo. Yet inevitably something will retrigger their anger, and the cycle will begin again. They shift back and forth between the "honeymoon phase" and the "abuse phase," which results in gaslighting, a key challenge for the victims of abuse.

*Gaslighting* is a type of emotional manipulation that results in others questioning their own experience, perception, memory, and even sanity. Once the seeds of doubt are sown, the victimized partner often sweeps things under the rug until, inevitably, the abuse happens again. And unfortunately, victims of abuse often want desperately for the abuse to end, but not the relationship or marriage, which keeps them from asserting their needs, boundaries, and consequences.

As clinicians, we must be on the alert for any abuse, ranging from subtle, covert, emotional abuse to overt and dangerous physical violence. At a minimum, we are there to educate our clients about the subtleties of emotional and verbal abuse. At the more extreme end, we are mandated to report any physical abuse or threat of harm to the client or others. Once we identify an abusive pattern, we must assess for the degree of danger, refer clients to appropriate support groups, create safety plans, and work to empower the victims, challenge the abusers, and begin the process of breaking the family out of the abusive cycle and creating healthy shifts.

## Characteristics of Abusive Partners

The abusive parent or partner may:

1. Humiliate, criticize, or demean family members
2. Yell or destroy others' property
3. Have an unpredictable temper
4. Embarrass family members around others
5. Ignore or stonewall family members
6. Blame others for their behavior
7. See others as property or objects
8. Physically and/or emotionally hurt or threaten to hurt others
9. Threaten suicide if their partner leaves
10. Threaten to take the children away if their partner leaves
11. Act jealous, possessive, and controlling of their partner
12. Control whom and when family members spend time with others
13. Limit access to money
14. Continuously check on their partner when with others

In response to these behaviors, victimized partners or children often feel:

1. Fearful of the abusive family member
2. That they are walking on eggshells
3. That they can't do anything right
4. That they may be crazy or overreacting
5. That they are numb, helpless, insecure, ashamed, and unlovable
6. Too embarrassed to have friends over
7. That they are controlled objects, without rights or identity

## The Cycle of Abuse

When working with families on issues related to domestic abuse, it is important to explain the cycle of abuse to the family and to differentiate it from healthy conflict, which consists of disagreement, apologies, and resolution. Healthy conflict involves sharing a complaint without becoming critical or contemptuous, avoiding escalation, coming to an agreement, and repairing any hurt feelings.

The cycle of abuse, on the other hand, looks like this:

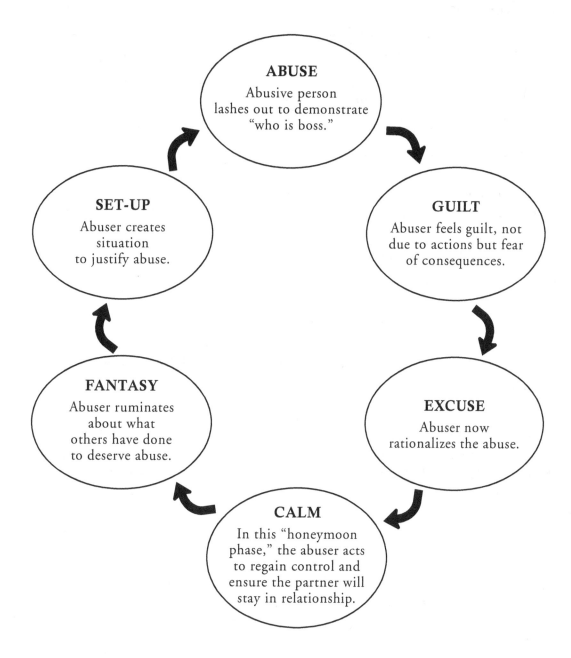

## The Impact of Verbal, Emotional, and Physical Domestic Abuse on the Family System

1. Physical, verbal, and emotional abuse impair safety in the home.
2. Family members live with fear, intimidation, and shame.
3. Family members fear being subjected to emotional or physical injury.
4. The abusive family member controls others through fear.
5. Children may act out, isolate, exhibit academic decline, self-harm, abuse substances, or struggle with low self-esteem.
6. The victimized partner may be caught between wanting the abuse to end and not wanting the relationship or marriage to end.

7. The victimized partner and children become isolated, depressed, and embarrassed.

8. The victimized partner may believe they are not worthy of love and develop low self-esteem.

9. The victimized partner may fear that if they leave, the abusive partner will gain some custody or have time alone with the children.

## Long-Term Family Goals

1. Family learns about the cycle of abuse and specific definitions of various types of abuse.

2. Family understands the overt, as well as the covert, manifestations of abuse.

3. Family learns skills to verbalize their needs, feelings, and expectations. This may include a written contract assuring no further abusive behavior, as well as the consequences if such behavior continues. The family is clear regarding the behaviors that violate the contract.

4. Assessment is made for any substance abuse in the family system.

5. If the abuse is physical, the abusive partner must live elsewhere during treatment.

6. If it is deemed safe for the family to remain in the same home, then expectations, boundaries, and de-escalation plans are set.

7. Safety plan with list of resources is created in the event of danger to family members.

8. Abusive partner seeks individual therapy to identify underlying triggers of abusive behavior and methods of self-soothing, emotional containment, and distress tolerance.

9. Abusive partner may be referred for psychiatric assessment.

On the following pages are four verbal, emotional, and physical domestic abuse assignments to give to your clients one week at a time. In session, explain the topic to them using the sample conversation I have provided as a guide, and then describe the assignments to them, answering any questions they may have. If necessary, help the family modify the assignments to be developmentally appropriate and understandable for all family members. Then send them home with the following assignments over the next four sessions, and process what they learned about verbal, emotional, and physical abuse, as well as their experience of sharing about the topic with one another, in each subsequent session.

> **Only give these assignments if you assess that it is safe for the family to complete them without therapeutic supervision and intervention. You must insist that family members respect boundaries and that they discontinue the assignments if emotions escalate.**

## Therapist Assignment Summaries

**Assignment #1:** *Verbal, Emotional, and Physical Domestic Abuse Family Conversation*
The questions in this conversation will help guide family members to express their feelings about the current family situation, as well as to ask any questions and express any needs they have. Feel free to adjust or add questions as seems fitting.

**Assignment #2:** *Dating Red Flags*
The purpose of this assignment is to educate preadolescents and adolescents, as well as young adult children, about the red flags of abusive behavior when dating.

**Assignment #3:** *Types of Verbal and Emotional Abuse*

The purpose of this assignment is to teach the family the various types of verbal and emotional abuse and to talk about why these behaviors are harmful.

**Assignment #4:** *Our Family Rights Contract*

The purpose of this assignment is for the family to read and agree to a contract of non-abusive behavior.

Once they have completed all four of the verbal, emotional, and physical domestic abuse assignments, and you have processed each in session, review the following goals to solidify their new understanding of this important topic.

## Verbal, Emotional, and Physical Domestic Abuse Assignments Wrap-Up

"Now that you have completed all four of the verbal, emotional, and physical domestic abuse assignments, and we have talked about them in session, we are going to review some of what you learned. Do you feel that you…"

1. Understand how abusive it is to humiliate, criticize, or demean one another?
2. Understand how frightening it is for others to experience an unpredictable temper or rage?
3. Realize how unfair it is to blame others for your behavior?
4. Understand how important it is to respect one another as individuals and not as objects that you own?
5. Understand the cycle of abuse and the specific types of verbal and emotional abuse?
6. Feel closer and safer now that you have agreed to and signed a family rights contract?

## Sample Conversation

Domestic abuse is a sensitive topic, and it is a critical topic for all families. *Abuse* is anything that is done to intentionally harm or injure another person, and all abuse is illegal and can result in criminal arrest. Abuse can involve a pattern of intimidation or frightening others, as well as actual verbal, emotional, or physical assault. Physical abuse involves any non-accidental force that results in injury or pain, though it can also include physical restraint and neglect.

Abuse can be confusing because it tends to be cyclical. Abusers may go long periods being nice, and then something triggers them and they act out abusively. Afterward, they may be regretful and might even apologize, and things may seem fine for a while, until the abuse happens again.

It can be really difficult when an abuser does something hurtful and then denies it or tells you that you're overreacting, and you begin to doubt your feelings. This is called gaslighting, and it is destructive. It's extremely important to understand what abusive behaviors are, to make sure that they are not occurring in your family, and if they are, that they stop.

# Questions to Explore with Family Members

1. (Parents) Do you think that your children are ever scared of you when you're angry?

   _____

   _____

2. Do any of you ever feel like you are walking on eggshells so no one in the family gets mad?

   _____

   _____

3. Does anyone ever feel like they can't do anything right at home?

   _____

   _____

4. Do any of you ever get upset at someone and then think maybe you're crazy or overreacting?

   _____

   _____

5. Are any of you ever too nervous to invite friends over because of a family member's temper?

   _____

   _____

6. Do you all feel that you have certain rights in the family?

   _____

   _____

I'm going to send you home today with one of four physical, emotional, and verbal domestic abuse assignments that are going to benefit you in three ways:

1. First, it is going to give you the opportunity to talk together about the harm of abusive behavior and why it is important to treat one another with respect.

2. Next, you are going to learn some of the red flags of abusive behavior in dating, as well as the various types of verbal and emotional abuse.

3. And finally, you are going to read and sign a family rights contract that clearly states the healthy behaviors you all agree to abide by in your family.

*Remember that you all are allowed to have the feelings you have.*
*Be kind and loving to one another.*

# Verbal, Emotional, and Physical Domestic Abuse Conversation

*Love is the child of freedom, never that of domination.*
—Erich Fromm

Create a comforting environment where you can have a loving conversation about the impact of abuse in your family. Make sure everyone is comfortable, turn your phones off, light a candle, and take a moment to close your eyes, take a few deep breaths, and then be present. You may choose a family member to take some notes or simply talk and listen.

1. Do we all agree that physical, verbal, or emotional abuse should never occur in our family?

_____

_____

_____

2. Why do you think it is so harmful and hurtful to treat one another abusively?

_____

_____

_____

3. (Parents to children) Do you ever feel afraid of us when we are disciplining you?

_____

_____

_____

4. (Parents to children) Do you feel like we are fair and respectful when we ask you to do something?

_____

_____

_____

5. Why do you think that name-calling is so hurtful?

_____

_____

_____

6. Do you ever feel that you're not allowed to have your own point of view?

_____

_____

_____

7. Why do you think it's important to receive a sincere apology when someone hurts you with something they say or do?

_____

_____

_____

8. Do you ever feel criticized or judged by anyone in our family?

_____

_____

_____

9. Do you agree that we should never have to experience angry outbursts or rages in our family?

_____

_____

_____

10. Why is it important that we all treat one another with respect, emotional support, encouragement, and goodwill?

_____

_____

_____

# Dating Red Flags

It's important that parents educate their adolescents about the traits of abusive partners. All too often, an abusive partner is extremely charming at first, pouring on affection and compliments, which makes it more difficult to see the transition to abusive behavior. By then, the victimized partner has developed feelings for their abuser, and a breakup seems devastating to your young teenager.

Draw a line to match the behavior with the term, and then discuss why this behavior is abusive. Have one family member take notes, and then share with your therapist in the next session.

| BEHAVIOR | ABUSE TERM |
|---|---|
| a. Compliments; intense attention | 1. "Shoulds" |
| b. "Where are you? Who are you with? I need your passwords" | 2. Isolating |
| c. Possessive; critical of friends; makes you feel guilty for seeing friends | 3. Monitoring |
| d. Tells you how you should cut your hair, how you should speak, and whom you should (or shouldn't) see | 4. Physical abuse |
| e. Withdraws when you don't do what they want; nice when you please them | 5. Manufacturing jealousy |
| f. Makes you think you are in trouble and/or that someone else likes them | 6. Criticism |
| g. Starts small arguments over things that don't make sense; gradually more extreme and confusing | 7. Hot/Cold |
| h. Focuses on what you are doing wrong | 8. Gaslighting |
| i. Confidence becomes arrogance | 9. Pick fights to test you |
| j. Denies your reality and makes you question your sanity | 10. Superiority |
| k. Slaps, bruises, or physically restrains you | 11. Love-bombing |

**Answer Key:**
a. 11, b. 3, c. 2, d. 1, e. 7, f. 5, g. 9, h. 6, i. 10, j. 8, k. 4

# Types of Verbal, Emotional, and Physical Domestic Abuse

Take turns reading the following examples of verbal and emotional abuse. Next, share as a group any experience you have had with types of abuse in your family or with others and why it was or would be hurtful.

1. **Withholding:** Relationships require intimacy and empathy. When someone withholds, they do not share their feelings and do not support their partner or family members in an empathic, caring way.

   Phrases such as: "There's nothing to talk about. What do you want me to say? You never let me talk."

2. **Discounting:** This is denying the reality and experience of others.

   Phrases such as: "You're too sensitive. You're jumping to conclusions. You blow everything out of proportion."

3. **Jokes:** Abusive joking does not feel funny because it is actually a way to disparage and demean others.

   Phrases such as: "You just can't take a joke. Boy, are you easily entertained. What else can you expect from a women/man/boy/girl?"

4. **Blocking and diverting:** This is a way to control a conversation, end communication, or keep from sharing information.

   Phrases such as: "You know what I meant. That's a lot of crap. You always have to be right. Did anybody ask you?"

5. **Accusing and blaming:** This is a way to blame others for one's own anger.

   Phrases such as: "This is all your fault. You made me do this. You were asking for it"

6. **Judging and criticizing:** These statements often begin with "you," may be said about you to others, or are disguised as helpful.

   Phrases such as: "You're too sensitive. He never sticks to anything. It would have been tastier if you added more salt."

7. **Threatening:** This manipulates others by triggering their worst fears.

   Phrases such as: "Do what I want or I'll leave. Do what I want or I'll divorce you. Do what I want or I'll hit you."

8. **Name-calling:** All name-calling is abusive. It is a way of demeaning and insulting others.

9. **Ordering:** This is a way of treating others like they are unequal and have no right to their say.

   Phrases such as: "Get in here and clean this up. You're not wearing that. We're not talking about that."

10. **Denial:** This is involves denying the reality of others, and it is extremely destructive.

    Phrases such as: "I never said that. You're getting upset over nothing. You've got to be crazy."

# Our Family Rights Contract

We agree that we all have the right to goodwill, encouragement, and emotional support. We have the right to our own point of view and to have our feelings acknowledged as real and valid. We have the right to clear and informative answers to our questions and to have our interests and work respected. When someone asks us to do things in the home or for one another, they do so in a respectful request instead of making any demands.

We all have the right to live without accusation, blame, personal jokes, name-calling, criticism, judgment, and any non-accidental physical force, and to receive a sincere apology for any such behaviors that occur.

And finally, our home must be a safe haven, free of any angry outbursts, rage, or threats of emotional, verbal, or physical abuse.

We all sign this contract with love and admiration for one another.

_____

_____

_____

_____

Date: _____

# 16

# Alcohol Abuse

## Therapist Preparation

Alcohol use disorder (AUD), often referred to as alcoholism, is a disease. According to the National Institute on Alcohol Abuse and Alcoholism, AUD is a "chronic relapsing brain disease characterized by compulsive alcohol use, loss of control over alcohol intake, and a negative emotional state when not using." Approximately 16 million people in the United States have AUD, including an estimated 623,000 adolescents aged 12 to 17.

AUD is a family disorder. Children growing up with an alcoholic parent are at greater risk of emotional problems and are more likely to experience neglect, as well as physical, verbal, or emotional abuse. Many children may also have a parent who enables the alcoholic family member and who is in denial about the systemic impact of the disease. Alcoholism destroys marriages and can create tension and conflict between all members who may have differing perspectives on whether the abusing parent has a problem.

As family therapists, we must assess for any signs of addiction. Clients may initially communicate this information as the reason they are seeking therapy, or we may discover it as we explore the family dynamics. When working with a family in which there is a member actively abusing alcohol, treatment begins by identifying the stage of addiction, breaking down any denial in the alcohol abuser and family members, and making any referrals for inpatient or outpatient treatment and support groups. If the alcohol abuser is currently sober yet not in true recovery, our work focuses on identifying and shifting dysfunctional patterns in the alcoholic family system.

## Five Stages of Change

1. **Pre-contemplation:** At this stage the addicted member does not believe they have a problem, is often defensive when confronted, and rationalizes their alcohol use. The goal for a clinician is to move the client toward contemplation by focusing on the consequences of their addiction, and consider a change.

2. **Contemplation:** At this stage the client is aware of the consequences of their alcohol abuse, yet may not be ready to make changes. The clinician will now weigh the costs and benefits of recovery, and begin to imagine a healthier life.

3. **Preparation:** At this stage the client has committed to change. The clinician will now help the client prepare to take action by exploring treatment options.

4. **Action:** At this stage the client is actively involved in recovery. The clinician will focus on coping strategies and communication skills as an adjunct to any program they are following.

5. **Maintenance/Recovery:** At this stage the client is sober and committed to ongoing recovery. The clinician will focus on helping the client avoid triggers that may lead to relapse, practicing stress management, and continuing to create a life of meaning and purpose.

# Impact on Children

One in four children under the age of 18 are dealing with the effects of living with a parent who abuses drugs or alcohol. According to Claudia Black, PhD, children in addicted homes are likely to take on one of four possible roles in order to cope:

1. The **responsible child** takes responsibility for the family and remains somewhat isolated from others. They learn to be self-disciplined and are goal-oriented leaders, yet they also struggle with an inability to relax or listen to others. They develop a need to be in control and fear making mistakes.

   *Parents can help this child by letting them know that it is okay to make mistakes, that they don't have to be the leader, and that the parent is the responsible one (not the child).*

2. The **adjuster** avoids and adjusts to chaotic situations. They learn to be easygoing and flexible, but they also fear making decisions or initiating actions, and they may lack direction.

   *Parents can help this child by emphasizing their strengths, including them in decision-making, and exploring their interests.*

3. The **placater** takes care of everyone. They learn to be good listeners and are caring and empathic, yet they also fear anger, develop a high tolerance for inappropriate behavior, and have trouble focusing on their own needs.

   *Parents can help this child by validating their worth, asking them about their feelings, and showing them that the parent is the responsible adult.*

4. The **act-out child** is often in trouble and has difficulty relating to others. They tend to be creative and honest, yet they have difficulty following directions, experience social problems, and struggle with anger.

   *Parents can help this child by setting limits, letting them know when their behavior is unacceptable, and validating them when they take responsibility for things.*

Children being raised by a parent with AUD may also experience the following emotions and behaviors:

- Guilt as a result of blaming themselves for the drinking
- Anxiety or depression
- Fear of tension or violence at home, or of the alcoholic parent harming themselves
- Feelings of helplessness
- Shame, resulting in a reluctance to have friends over due to the fear that they might see the parent intoxicated
- Anger at the alcoholic parent or the enabling parent
- Confusion and difficulty coping with the inconsistent emotions of the alcoholic parent
- Isolation due to difficulty trusting or getting close to others
- Academic decline, truancy
- Oppositional or conduct-disordered behavior
- Physical illness
- Substance abuse
- Aggressive and risk-taking behaviors

## The Impact of Alcohol Abuse on the Family System

1. The abuse of alcohol by one or more family members interferes with the overall functioning of the family.

2. The abuse of alcohol by a parent creates tension in the marriage or relationship and results in an inequitable division of responsibilities.

3. Verbal or physical abuse or intimidation may occur due to alcohol abuse.

4. Family members may be in denial of any problem with alcohol abuse.

5. Financial problems may occur due to compulsive spending, missed work, or the loss of job.

6. Children may act out due to tension in the home, lack of structure, and depression in the non-substance-abusing parent.

7. The modeling of alcohol abuse in the home may result in early substance-abusing patterns among children.

8. Family members experience shame and secrecy due to alcohol abuse in the home.

9. When an adolescent is abusing alcohol, siblings may find that their needs are not attended to, as parents are preoccupied by the crisis. The siblings may then engage in inappropriate behaviors to get attention, schoolwork may suffer, or they may become depressed.

## Long-Term Family Goals

1. Family members may organize an intervention to share their realization that their family member is abusing alcohol and their need for them to seek treatment.

2. The family member who is abusing alcohol accepts that they have an AUD and seeks treatment.

3. Family members participate in the recovery program, share the emotional impact of the alcohol abuse, express their need for the affected member to maintain sobriety and recovery, and set consequences should they relapse.

4. Alcohol abuser seeks therapy to understand the impact of previous life experiences, to recognize triggers to cravings, and to develop coping skills to maintain sobriety.

5. Family members learn what behaviors they may have engaged in to protect the abusing member, commit to no longer supporting the behavior, and process the impact of living in an alcoholic family system.

6. Family members attend Al-Anon or another support group to help them move through their own recovery.

7. Family members begin to reconnect and feel more hopeful about the future as they all move through recovery.

On the following pages are four alcohol abuse assignments to give to your clients one week at a time. In session, explain the topic to them using the sample conversation I have provided as a guide, and then describe the assignments to them, answering any questions they may have. If necessary, help the family modify the assignments to be developmentally appropriate and understandable for all family members. Then send them home with the following assignments over the next four sessions, and process what they have learned about the impact of alcohol abuse on the family system, as well as their experience of sharing about the topic with one another, in each subsequent session.

**Only give these assignments if you assess that it is safe for the family to complete them without therapeutic supervision and intervention. You must insist that family members respect boundaries and that they discontinue the assignments if emotions escalate.**

## Therapist Assignment Summaries

**Assignment #1:** *Alcohol Abuse Family Conversation*

The questions in this conversation will help guide family members to express their feelings about the current family situation, as well as to ask any questions and express any needs they have. Feel free to adjust or add questions as seems fitting.

**Assignment #2:** *Practicing "I" Statements*

The purpose of this assignment is for family members to practice using "I" statements to express their feelings in a nonconfrontational manner so they can be heard by the alcohol abuser without defensiveness.

**Assignment #3:** *My Role in the Alcoholic Family System*

The purpose of this assignment is for each child in the family to identify the role that they may have taken on to cope in this family system

**Assignment #4:** *Drawing My Feelings*

In this three-part assignment, family members will explore their feelings through the use of art. The purpose of the first exercise is for family members to draw and share the highs and lows in their life and their vision for the next peak. Next, they will engage in a fun exercise that involves scribbling on paper and turning the scribble into something meaningful. From this, they will have a conversation about how the messiness of life can be transformed with intention, support, and patience. Finally, they will write a list of feelings they have in corresponding colors and then place them on a heart.

Once they have completed all four of the alcohol abuse assignments, and you have processed each in session, review the following goals to solidify their new understanding of this important topic.

## Alcohol Abuse Assignments Wrap-Up

"Now that you have completed all four of the alcohol abuse assignments, and we have talked about them in session, we are going to review some of what you learned. Do you feel that you…"

1. Understand that AUD is a disease of the brain that affects emotional, physical, and psychological health?
2. Are allowed to share your feelings with your family members?
3. Are aware of how your behaviors and feelings were affected by the addiction in the family?
4. (Children) Can expect your parents to be responsible adults so you can focus on being a child or adolescent?
5. Did not cause the addiction, nor can you change or control it?
6. Have no reason to feel any shame for having a family member who struggles with addiction?
7. Are not responsible for making excuses for a family member who is abusing alcohol?
8. Deserve to live in a healthy home where parents take responsibility for being functional, present, sober adults?

## Sample Conversation

When a family member is struggling with alcohol abuse, it affects the whole family. We call it alcohol use disorder, or AUD, and it is actually considered a disease of the brain. It causes people to lose their ability to control their use of alcohol, affects them physically and mentally, and often creates tension and conflict in the home.

Another thing that can happen is that other family members may take on responsibilities that they shouldn't have to in order to make up for things that the alcohol abuser is not doing. This becomes too much to continue, and eventually family members also become both mentally and physically ill. It can be really hard to admit that your loved one has an addiction, and you may feel scared to confront them or guilty if you do. It's important to be able to be honest and to let your loved one know that they need to find sobriety and recovery. Only then will you be able to repair as a family, and I am here to help with that.

# Questions to Explore with Family Members

1. How has [*name of family member*]'s alcohol abuse impacted you?

_____

_____

_____

2. Have any of you been able to voice your concerns?

_____

_____

_____

3. Have you ever felt frightened or embarrassed when they are intoxicated?

_____

_____

_____

4. Has it ever kept you from inviting friends over?

_____

_____

_____

5. Have you ever worried about their physical health or that they will have an accident because of alcohol?

_____

_____

_____

6. Has there been any tension among the rest of you because you don't all see this as a problem?

_____

_____

_____

7. (AUD member) How are you feeling about your loved ones' responses?

_____

_____

_____

8. (AUD member) How has the alcohol abuse affected you and your life?

_____

_____

_____

9. (AUD member) How committed are you to becoming sober and seeking recovery? Or how has your experience of being sober and working on recovery been for you?

_____

_____

_____

10. Is there anything you would like to share with your family right now about this road to recovery and reconnection?

_____

_____

_____

I'm going to send you home today with one of four alcohol abuse assignments that are going to benefit you in three ways:

1. First, it is going to give you the opportunity to talk together about the impact of alcohol abuse on your family.

2. Next, you are going to practice using "I" statements to share how you have experienced your loved one's alcohol abuse.

3. And finally, you are going to use art to explore the highs and lows in your life and what you want going forward.

*Remember that you all are allowed to have the feelings you have.*
*Be kind and loving to one another.*

# Alcohol Abuse Conversation

*Addiction begins with the hope that something*
*"out there" can instantly fill up the emptiness inside.*
—Jean Kilbourne

Create a comforting environment where you can have a loving conversation about the impact of alcohol abuse in the family. Make sure everyone is comfortable, turn your phones off, light a candle, and take a moment to close your eyes, take a few deep breaths, and then be present. You may choose a family member to take some notes or simply talk and listen.

1. How are you all feeling right now as we talk about [*name of family member*]'s alcohol abuse?

_____

_____

_____

2. Do you feel comfortable telling [*name of family member*] how their alcohol abuse has affected you?

_____

_____

_____

3. How do you think it has impacted us as a family?

_____

_____

_____

4. Has it affected any of you at school, at work, or with friends?

_____

_____

_____

5. Do you ever feel anxious or depressed about it?

_____

_____

_____

6. Do you understand that it is a brain disease, and that [*name of family member*] needs help just as they would if it were any other physical disease?

_____

_____

_____

7. (AUD member) How do you feel knowing that alcohol is a brain disease?

_____

_____

_____

8. (AUD member) How has alcohol abuse affected your ability to manage your life and relationships?

_____

_____

_____

9. (AUD member) Is there anything you would like to say to help your family feel supported and hopeful?

_____

_____

_____

10. Do all of us understand that we did not cause this and that we can't control it?

_____

_____

_____

11. Can you each say one thing that you are hopeful for when [*name of family member*] becomes sober and healthy?

_____

_____

_____

# Practicing "I" Statements

In order for your family to recover from the effects of alcohol abuse, it is necessary to share how you have experienced it. Using "I" statements is a way to share how *you* feel without attacking or judging and for your loved one to hear without becoming defensive.

Complete the following statements openly, honestly, and lovingly. Then take turns reading them aloud to the alcohol abuser in the family.

1. I see you _____ .

2. I feel _____ .

3. I hope _____ .

4. I worry about _____ .

5. I was hurt when _____ .

6. I miss _____ .

7. I was angry when _____ .

8. I expect _____ .

9. I have been affected by this in these ways: _____

_____

_____

10. I want you to know that what I love about you is _____

_____

_____

# My Role in the Alcoholic Family System

Children in homes with addiction often develop a particular role in the family. Read through the following descriptions and put a check mark beside any that you feel fit your personality. Then share your results, and read the suggestions below regarding your particular role with your family. Feel free to respectfully and lovingly talk about how this role may affect you and your life.

1. Take responsibility for the family

_____ Feel somewhat isolated from others

_____ Self-disciplined

_____ Goal-oriented

_____ Take on leadership

_____ Have trouble relaxing

_____ Hard on yourself when you make a mistake or fail

*If you have one or more of these traits, you may have taken on the role of "**The Responsible Child**." It's important to know that it is okay to make mistakes, that you don't always have to be the leader, and that you are allowed to be a child and let your parents be the adults.*

2. Avoids conflict

_____ Easygoing

_____ Flexible

_____ Have trouble making decisions

_____ Prefer to follow rather than lead

_____ Adjust fairly easily to chaotic situations

_____ May lack direction

*If you have one or more of these traits, you may have taken on the role of "**The Adjuster**." It's important to focus on your own strengths, to give yourself permission to make your own decisions, and to explore things that interest you and not just things that interest others.*

3. Takes care of everyone

_____ Good listener

_____ Caring

_____ Empathic

_____ Fear anger

_____ Have trouble focusing on yourself

_____ More likely to tolerate inappropriate behavior from others

*If you have more of these traits, you may have taken on the role of "**The Placater**." It's important to know your own worth, to expect others to care about your feelings, and to expect your parents to be responsible for their own feelings and decisions.*

4. Often in trouble

_____ Have difficulty relating to others

_____ Creative

_____ Have trouble following directions

_____ Anger easily

_____ Honest

_____ Struggle in social situations

*If you have more of these traits, you may have taken on the role of "**The Acting-Out Child**." It's important for you to know and respect the limits and boundaries inside and outside your family, to know that you deserve to have your strengths and efforts validated, and to expect others to care about your feelings.*

All children in homes with addiction need to know that:

- It's okay to say no.

- Your needs matter.

- You deserve to be listened to.

- Others should never take advantage of you.

- You should not feel any shame or guilt due to your parent's addiction.

- You are enough just as you are, and you are worthy of love.

# Drawing My Feelings

**Materials:**

- Large poster board for each family member

- Large sheet of paper for each family member

- Crayons

### 1. Peaks and Valleys

Cut your poster board in half and use one of the halves to draw a series of mountain peaks and valleys. At each peak, write a happy memory from your life, and in the valleys, write some of the more difficult times. Finally, write some of your hopes and dreams at the top of the last peak. Then share your peaks and valleys with your family.

### 2. From Chaos to Clarity

Choose a crayon, and get ready to use the second half of your poster board. When everyone is ready, have one family member count to three, and everyone should scribble on their board for three more seconds and STOP.

Now take a little time to look at your scribble and, using any other crayons you like, color in the various shapes in the scribble to create a design or picture.

Share your artwork with your family, explaining how it felt to create something new from the scribble.

### 3. A Heart Full of Feelings

Draw a large heart on a sheet of paper. Along the side of the sheet, write a list of the feelings you have had through your experience in the alcoholic family system, using a crayon that represents each feeling. Next, color your heart using all the colors that represent the feelings you have been experiencing. Then share your heart and feelings with your family.

# 17

# Chronic Illness

## Therapist Preparation

According to the American Association for Marriage and Family Therapy, there are approximately 35 million Americans with a chronic mental or physical illness. These illnesses may impact an individual's daily life or include periods of remission and relapse, yet they almost always affect the family as a whole. Roles and routines often need to change, and all family members experience a new norm to some degree or another.

The impact of chronic illness is determined, in part, by the developmental stage of the family system and its individual members, as well as the role of the particular family member who has become ill. If a parent is ill, they will require additional support and responsibility-taking by a partner or extended family members, and children often experience anxiety as the parent is less available. If a child is ill, the parental focus tends to shift to the care of that child, and the other children, if any, are forced to adapt to that change.

Often an emotional roller coaster begins as family members may experience, shock, anxiety, depression, guilt, resentment, helplessness, confusion, and denial. Financial stress may occur if one parent is forced to leave a job due to their own illness or to care for a sick child, as well as from mounting medical bills. Couples often experience tension due to anxiety or differing opinions about medical care and decisions. And siblings may act out as a result of changes in routine and the availability of parental attention.

As psychotherapists, we need to guide the family to identify and express their various feelings and concerns and normalize their experience. We help by educating them about the stages of grief as a new norm evolves, by referring them to various support groups, and by developing new routines, boundaries, and expectations. We also help by encouraging them to engage in fun activities and rituals in order to maintain a family identity that is not solely defined by that of a chronically ill parent or child.

## Self-Care for a Parent with Chronic Illness

When working with a chronically ill parent, you can share the following guidelines to promote their self-care:

1. Maintain balance by allowing yourself to carve out time for you, time to be a parent, and time to be a partner. Making time for friendships, hobbies, and alone time are important and help you to maintain an identity apart from your illness.
2. Give yourself permission to set limits. Whether you are playing with the children, spending time with your partner, or working on a project, allow yourself to stop when you need rest.

3. Keep a gratitude journal. Write a list of things you are grateful for that you can refer to when the emotional heaviness of your illness sets in. It will help you challenge catastrophic thoughts and regain a sense of hopefulness. Add a thought or two to the list each day.

4. Accept a new normal. Acceptance is the final stage of grief, and it is an important stage in forming a new perspective and a new lens.

5. Set boundaries with play areas in the home. Keeping the mess to a minimum and setting expectations that the children will help clean up is another important part of your self-care.

6. Seek psychotherapy, join support groups, and ask for help from friends and family. Reaching out for help and support is a strength, not a weakness. It is a tool that will help you maintain a life of meaning and purpose despite your chronic illness.

## Managing with a Chronically Ill Child:

When working with a family in which there is a child with a chronic illness, you can share the following guidelines to assist the family in navigating their care:

1. Keep the line of communication open. Help your child to label their feelings and allow them to share openly.

2. Maintain a predictable and consistent schedule, and incorporate healthy distractions like time with friends and fun activities.

3. Use appropriate discipline and expectations. Your child is still a child and needs to feel that way. Having rules and appropriate consequences is important, as is avoiding any power struggles due to frustration, or overprotectiveness due to anxiety.

4. Praise your child for cooperating with treatment. Compliance with medications and treatments can be challenging, so positive reinforcement is essential.

5. Keep an open line of communication with teachers and any other educational support systems.

6. Emphasize the child's unique talents and strengths and allow them to explore.

## The Impact of Chronic Illness on the Family System

1. Family members are overwhelmed by strong emotions, such as guilt, anger, sadness, fear, and anxiety.

2. Some family members may struggle with denial.

3. If the family member is a child, parents may become consumed with the child's medical care at the expense of all other aspects of life.

4. If the family member is a parent, children may fear the loss of the ill parent, as well as the other parent becoming ill too.

5. As a result of anxiety and grief, children may act out and have difficulty with school, sleep, appetite, and social interactions.

6. Family members may differ in their opinions about medical treatment, creating tension and frustration.

7. Daily routines change, family members take on additional responsibilities, and extended family and friends are asked to help.

8. The family may experience financial stress due to medical expenses and may require one working parent to leave a job to care for the ill member of the family.

## Long-Term Family Goals

1. Family members learn to express their feelings and needs in therapy and ask any questions they have about prognosis and plans.

2. The ill family member is able to share their feelings and needs and, if age-appropriate, have a sense of power and control over medical decisions.

3. The family is educated about the stages of grief.

4. Efforts are made to keep the ill family member from feeling isolated and powerless.

5. The ill family member seeks individual therapy to process feelings about the possible uncertainty and unpredictability of the illness.

6. The family is able to ask for help from extended family or friends.

7. Family members have access to support groups and educational materials to help cope with the trauma to the family.

8. The family is able to regain and maintain healthy boundaries, structure, and a sense of normalcy when manageable.

9. Family members nurture their own self-care.

10. Parents communicate with children's teachers about the family health crisis.

On the following pages are two chronic illness assignments to give to your clients one week at a time. In session, explain the topic to them using the sample conversation I have provided as a guide, and then describe the assignments to them, answering any questions they may have. If necessary, help the family modify the assignments to make them developmentally appropriate and understandable for all family members. Then send them home with the following assignments over the next two sessions, and process what they learned about the impact of chronic illness on the family system, as well as their experience of sharing about the topic with one another, in each subsequent session.

## Therapist Assignment Summaries

**Assignment #1:** *Chronic Illness Family Conversation*

The questions in this conversation will help guide family members to express their feelings about the current family situation, as well as to ask any questions and express any needs they have. Feel free to adjust or add questions as seems fitting.

**Assignment #2:** *Calming with Creativity Assignments*

The purpose of this assignment is to offer five methods of tapping into and sharing feelings:

1. *Drawing My Feelings*: Helps family members tap into and express feelings

2. *Dancing on Paper*: Helps them practice self-soothing

3. *Calming Collage*: Allows them to explore what makes them feel calm and to feel like a cohesive family unit

4. *Me as a Tree*: Taps into feelings of strength, solidity, and community as members see the family as a beautiful forest

5. *I Have an Illness, but I Am Not My Illness*: Allows the chronically ill family member to see themselves as a whole person who is not defined solely by their illness

Once the family has completed both of the chronic illness assignments, and you have processed each in session, review the following goals to solidify their new understanding of this important topic.

## Chronic Illness Assignments Wrap-Up

"Now that you have completed both of the chronic illness assignments, and we have talked about them in session, we are going to review some of what you have learned. Do you feel that you..."

1. Are more in touch with the feelings you have had throughout this experience?
2. Are more able to calm yourself down with art, music, or visualization?
3. Are more able to talk about your feelings and ask for what you need?

## Sample Conversation

There are approximately 35 million people with a chronic illness in this country. The symptoms or degree of illness may be different, but they always affect the family to some degree, as I'm sure you know. Family routines might change, and life just begins to feel different in certain ways.

You may each experience it a little differently depending on your age and what else is going on in your life, but you are all affected in some way. You have probably found that sometimes you feel calm about it, and other times you are worried, sad, or even irritable. It can feel like you are on an emotional roller coaster, and that is actually very normal.

# Questions to Explore with Family Members

1. How did you feel when you first heard that [*name of family member*] had an illness?

   _____

   _____

2. Have you been able to ask questions when you have had them?

   _____

   _____

3. Has it ever made you sad or worried?

   _____

   _____

4. How has life at home changed since [*name of family member*] has been ill?

   _____

   _____

5. (To the ill family member) What sort of changes have you noticed in your life since you have been ill?

   _____

   _____

6. (To the ill family member) Is there anything that you have needed from your family that you haven't felt comfortable asking for?

   _____

   _____

7. (To the ill family member) Are you able to share your feelings with your family?

_____

_____

I'm going to send you home today with one of two chronic illness assignments that are going to benefit you in three ways:

1. First, it is going to give you the opportunity to talk together about the impact of chronic illness on your family.

2. Next, you are going to do a number of creative assignments to tap into your feelings, self-soothe, and access your strengths.

3. Finally, your chronically ill family member will practice seeing themself as a whole and wonderful person.

*Remember that you all are allowed to have the feelings you have.*
*Be kind and loving to one another.*

# Chronic Illness Conversation

*I long to accomplish a great and noble task, but it is my chief
duty to accomplish small tasks as if they were great and noble.*
—Helen Keller

Create a comforting environment where you can have a loving conversation about the impact of chronic illness in the family. Make sure everyone is comfortable, turn your phones off, light a candle, and take a moment to close your eyes, take a few deep breaths, and then be present. You may choose a family member to take some notes, or simply talk and listen.

1. What was it like for you when you heard that [*name of family member*] was ill?

_____

_____

_____

2. What worries do you have about it?

_____

_____

_____

3. (To the ill family member) Do you feel like we have been supportive to you?

_____

_____

_____

4. (To the ill family member) Do you feel like you can tell us how you are feeling?

_____

_____

_____

5. (To the ill family member) Do we, or does anyone else, ever say things about your illness, or about how you are feeling, that upset you?

_____

_____

_____

6. Do you feel like our family routines have changed a lot?

_____

_____

_____

7. Is there anything that we can do to make things feel more normal at home?

_____

_____

_____

8. Do any of you ever feel angry about this?

_____

_____

_____

9. What sort of things would you like us to do more of as a family?

_____

_____

_____

10. (To the ill child) Is there anything that we parents do that upsets you? Are we overprotective?

_____

_____

_____

11. (To the ill parent) Are you giving yourself permission to have time for yourself?

_____

_____

_____

12. How would you describe the "new normal" in our family?

_____

_____

_____

13. Name one thing that you are grateful for at this moment.

_____

_____

_____

# Calming with Creativity
## Drawing My Feelings

**Materials:**

- Paper

- Colored markers

1. Close your eyes and think about a time when you were worried about your illness.

2. Now, open your eyes, take a colored marker, and draw what that worry looked like to you.

3. Next, close your eyes and think about a time when you felt angry about your illness.

4. Now, open your eyes, take a marker, and draw what that anger looked like.

5. Next, close your eyes and think about a time when you felt sad about your illness.

6. Now, open your eyes, take a marker, and draw what that sadness looked like.

7. Next, close your eyes and think about a time you were happy with your family.

8. Now, open your eyes, take a marker, and draw what that happiness looked like.

9. Finally, close your eyes and think about yourself feeling healthy.

10. Now, open your eyes, take a marker, and draw what your healthiness looked like.

# Calming with Creativity
## Dancing on Paper

**Materials:**

- Poster boards

- Tempera or watercolor paint

1. Have a parent choose a calm piece of music that all family members will enjoy.

2. Begin the music, close your eyes for a moment, and really listen. Think about the word *calm*. Notice how your body feels when it is calm. Notice your mind settle down. Notice your breathing slowing down.

3. Then open your eyes and begin to paint what the calm music sounds like to you.

4. Next, share your paintings with your family and describe how you felt as you interpreted the calm music with paint.

# Calming with Creativity
## Calming Collage

**Materials:**

- Large poster board

- Magazines

- Scissors

- Glue

1. Have each family member tear or cut out pictures from magazines that represent *calmness* to them.

2. Work together as a family to create a collage of these pictures by gluing them on the poster board.

3. When the collage is complete, admire the calming family collage that you have created together.

4. Keep it nearby to look at when you need to feel close and calm as a family.

# Calming with Creativity
## Me as a Tree

**Materials:**

- Large sheet of paper for each person

- Markers, crayons, or paint

1. Close your eyes and think of yourself as a strong, tall tree.

2. Notice how you feel, and notice the shape and color of your leaves.

3. Notice how deep your roots are. Notice the length of your branches. Notice the look of your bark. Are you alone or in a forest?

4. Now draw yourself as a tree. Use any colors and shapes that represent you, and give your tree a name.

5. When you are finished, share your tree with your family.

6. Finally, place all your tree drawings side by side, and name your new strong, beautiful family forest.

# I Have an Illness, but I Am Not My Illness

**Materials:**

- Large sheet of paper

- Markers, crayons, or paint

1. On the left side of the paper, draw yourself. Use colors that reflect how you feel emotionally and physically.

2. Next, write a list of your strengths, your positive traits, and anything you like about yourself.

3. Finally, draw yourself on the right side of the page, using colors that represent all of your strengths and positive traits.

4. Then share your drawings with your family. Notice any difference in the drawing that depicts your strengths and positive traits. THIS IS YOU. You are not defined by your illness.

5. Keep this drawing in your mind when you are feeling your worst as a reminder of who you are as a whole person.

# 18

# Sexuality and Gender Identity

## Therapist Preparation

In these modern times, almost everyone knows, has met, or has a family member who is part of the LGBTQ+ community. As of 2018, Gallup reported:

- 4.5 percent of Americans self-identify as gay, lesbian, or bisexual.
- 11 percent report some same-sex attractions.
- 0.7 percent are transgender, 2 in 300 of which are children.
- 4 percent identify as nonbinary.
- 1 percent identify as asexual.
- 1 in 5 have participated in consensual non-monogamous relationships.
- At least half of all gay couples are non-monogamous.
- At least half of all non-heterosexual people are bisexual/pansexual/sexually fluid.

Whether or not we are working specifically with LGTBQ+ people, it is essential that we, as psychotherapists, have some knowledge and education in order to be respectful with current pronouns, terms, lifestyles, perspectives, and developmental stages. Begin a first session by asking clients their name and pronouns, such as he/him/his, she/her/hers, or they/them/theirs.

We must also assume that all parts of healthy sexual diversity are non-pathological, and we must be sensitive to some of the inherent challenges LGBTQ+ people may face in society.

According to the National Association for Mental Health (NAMI), lesbian, gay, and bisexual adults are more than twice as likely as heterosexual adults to experience a mental health condition. LGBTQ+ people are at higher risk of suicidal thoughts and attempts than the general population, and high school students who are gay, lesbian, or bisexual are five times more likely to attempt suicide than their heterosexual peers. About 77 percent of transgender children experience mistreatment in grades K–12, and 54 percent are verbally abused. In general, gender-nonconforming boys are the most likely to be bullied. In addition, 48 percent of transgender adults report that they have considered suicide in the past 12 months, compared to 4 percent of the general population, and they are also more than twice as likely as heterosexual persons to experience mental illness.

According to a study by Ilan Meyer, PhD, sex- and gender-diverse populations experience unique and hostile stressors, which he refers to as "minority stress." Interestingly, his study also showed that many of the mental health disorders that these individuals struggle with disappear once they have positive care, and the suicide rate among transgender children is also greatly reduced with family support. This again makes it imperative that we as clinicians help families to accept and support their sex- and gender-diverse loved ones and help them to live healthy, purposeful lives.

LGBTQ+ children often view their parents as being non-accepting of their sexuality or gender identity at first, which often stems from parents desire to protect their children. We must validate the parent's fears and, at the same time, recognize that if they are in our office, they must be somewhat open to accepting and getting help. It's important to be aware of conflicts that may result from religious beliefs, as well as concern among parents that the stigma their child faces will be extended to them as well (referred to as "courtesy stigma"). We must also acknowledge the possibility that the parent is living with the unknown as their child explores their own uncertainty about their identity.

The following guidelines can help you when working with parents around issues related to their child's sexuality or gender identity:

1. Most parents love their children and want to be able to accept them.
2. Understand that parents are often shocked to learn about their child's sexual or gender orientation.
3. Parents need to grieve the vision they had of their child and their future. This should not be done in front of the child but with the therapist.
4. Process any feelings of self-blame.
5. Help the child to be patient with their parents as they learn and come to terms with their feelings.
6. Parents will need education on the LGBTQ+ community and specific health issues related to this community.
7. Guide parents toward support groups with other parents.

> **Most parents' first reaction will not be their last reaction.**

## Important Terms

- **Affirmed gender:** The gender by which an individual wishes to be known rather than the one they were assigned at birth
- **Asexual:** A sexual orientation generally characterized by a lack of sexual attraction or desire for partnered sexuality
- **Bisexual:** An individual who is physically, romantically, and/or emotionally attracted to more than one gender
- **Cisgender:** Gender assigned at birth matches one's identity
- **Gay:** Describes people whose enduring physical, romantic, and/or emotional attractions are to people of the same gender (Note: The term *homosexual* is outdated and considered derogatory and offensive by many LGBTQ+ people.)
- **Gender expression:** Refers to how you present to the outside world
- **Gender fluid:** A desire to remain flexible about gender identity
- **Gender identity:** Refers to who you feel you are
- **Lesbian:** A term often preferred for women whose enduring physical, romantic, and/or emotional attraction is to other women

- **Pansexual:** Someone who is physically, romantically, and/or emotionally attracted to people regardless of gender
- **Sexual orientation:** Refers to whom you are attracted
- **Transgender:** An umbrella term that covers anyone who does not believe that their internal experience of gender and their authentic gender identity match their outside expression

## Principles of Sex- and Gender-Diverse Affirmative Therapy

According to Margaret Nichols, PhD, the following principles should guide sex- and gender-diverse affirmative therapy:

1. Recognize and respect sex and gender diversity as a normal, universal, and non-pathological part of the human experience.
2. Commit to being knowledgeable about the sex and gender diversity of your clients and to keeping current.
3. Commit to examining your own internal biases and prejudices about sex- and gender-diverse people.
4. Advocate and support the development of authentic, self-defined sex and gender identity for all children, adolescents, and adults.
5. Consider any attempts by a professional to alter a client's sex or gender identity to align with socially stereotypical norms to be harmful and unethical, even if the client asks for it.
6. Understand the important role that family, school, medical practices, and spiritual, recreational, and community organizations play in the well-being of sex- and gender-diverse individuals.
7. Advocate for and intervene on the behalf of sex- and gender-diverse clients with these institutions.
8. Understand the concept of minority stress and its impact on sex- and gender-diverse clients.
9. Educate others about the needs of sex- and gender-diverse clients.
10. Be knowledgeable about other resources available to sex- and gender-diverse clients, and facilitate access to these resources.

## Developmental Stages of Sex- and Gender-Diverse People

In addition, Margaret Nichols, PhD, has identified several developmental stages through which LGBTQ+ individuals progress:

1. Recognition of sexual or gender-related desires: At this stage, identity may come into question due to thoughts, feelings, physical reactions, and experiences.
2. Recognition that these desires make them different: At this stage, there may be a feeling of being out of place. They may begin to socially distance themselves, may see their desires as unacceptable, and may try to inhibit their behavior.
3. Confusion or denial: At this stage, feelings and desires may be denied despite evidence to the contrary. They may avoid situations to explore their identity, or they may search for information.
4. Identity acceptance/coming out to self: At this stage, acceptance and exploration of identity may occur. There may be more interaction with the LGBTQ+ community and preference

for that environment. They may now begin to identify as LGBTQ+ in private yet not communicate this in public.

5. Coming out to others: At this stage, one identifies as LGBTQ+ in public as well. The individual's identity is potentially seen as more legitimate by coming out to others.

6. Affiliation with others like them: At this stage, the individual clearly identifies as LGBTQ+ and may prefer this community to the heterosexual/cisgender community.

7. Identity pride: At this stage, there is total alignment with private and public identities. There is pride and acceptance of identity and, at times, interest in public activism as well.

8. Integration into total self: At this stage, there is often more connection to the heterosexual/cisgender community as well as the LGBTQ+ community. LGBTQ+ identity is no longer the sole defining identity. The individual now integrates this identity into many other aspects of their overall identity.

## The Impact of Sexual and/or Gender Diversity on the Family System

1. A family member shares that they are LGBTQ+.
2. This is often met with mixed emotions, including anger, denial, sadness, guilt, fear, grief, and acceptance.
3. Parents may blame themselves.
4. Family members may fear they will be impacted by "courtesy stigma."
5. Family members may ostracize the LGBTQ+ member and show no interest in their lives or their friends.
6. LGBTQ+ member is at a higher risk of developing a mental health disorder without family support.
7. LGBTQ+ member may experience harassment at school and need support from family and other support systems.
8. LGBTQ+ member may be impatient with parents.

## Long-Term Family Goals

1. Parents and family members become educated about their loved one's sexuality or gender identity.
2. Parents become educated about any medical procedures should their loved one transition at some point.
3. Family resolves any conflicts around religion.
4. Family participates in therapy to work through the process of acceptance and seek individual therapy if needed.
5. Parents and family members reach acceptance and are supportive.
6. Parents let go of any guilt or blame, and they work through grief.
7. LGBTQ+ member is patient with the family's process of acceptance.
8. External support systems are put in place, such as local LGBTQ+ resource centers, student-run Gender-Sexuality Alliance (GSA) clubs, HealthyChildren.org, "It Gets Better Project," Nami.org, Glad.org, and the Institute for Personal Growth, which can be found at www.ipgcounseling.com.

9. Children who are significantly different from their parents need to connect with others who share their identity and therefore find that peer-support groups are essential.

On the following pages are two sex and gender identity assignments to give to your clients one week at a time. In session, explain the topic to them using the sample conversation I have provided as a guide, and then describe the assignments to them, answering any questions they may have. If necessary, help the family modify the assignments to make them developmentally appropriate and understandable for all family members. Then send them home with the following assignments over the next two sessions, and process what they learned about the impact of sex and gender diversity on the family system, as well as their experience of sharing about the topic with one another, in each subsequent session.

## Therapist Assignment Summaries

**Assignment #1:** *Sexuality and Gender Identity Family Conversation*

The questions in this conversation will help guide family members to express their feelings about the current family situation, as well as to ask any questions and express any needs they have. Feel free to adjust or add questions as seems fitting.

**Assignment #2:** *Our Family Acceptance Plan*

The purpose of this assignment is to strengthen the family commitment to love, support, and accept the sex- and gender-diverse family member.

Once they have completed both of the sex and gender diversity assignments, and you have processed each in session, review the following goals in order to solidify their new understanding of this important topic.

## Sexuality and Gender Diversity Assignments Wrap-Up

"Now that you have completed both of the sex and gender diversity assignments, and we have talked about them in session, we are going to review some of what you have learned. Do you feel that you..."

1. Understand the importance of loving, supporting, and accepting your sex- or gender-diverse family member?
2. Understand that your loved one's sexuality or gender identity is not an illness or in any way pathological?
3. Have a responsibility to educate yourself about your loved one's sexuality or gender identity?
4. May take some time to really understand this but must always be respectful and loving?
5. Understand the meanings of *gender identity, gender expression, sexual orientation,* and any other important terms?
6. Have a responsibility to participate in family therapy to help your loved one feel valued and accepted and to keep your family connected and close?
7. Are able to ask questions or express your feelings and concerns whenever you need to?
8. Are, first and foremost a wonderful family, that will always love one another unconditionally and have so much to look forward to?

## Sample Conversation

(This can clearly be a very difficult and emotional subject to broach with a family, so please use your therapeutic expertise to incorporate the information I have shared and adjust the conversation as you see fit.)

In these modern times, almost everyone knows, has met, or has a family member who identifies as LGBTQ+. When a family learns that one of their family members also has a different sexuality or gender identity, it's very common to be shocked at first and to then experience an array of feelings. And even though parents may seem non-accepting at first, it's often because they want to protect their child.

It's completely normal to have all sorts of feelings, and I am here to help you understand what you're thinking and feeling, learn how to express those thoughts and feelings as a family, and move through this process of accepting your loved one. We know from research that having a diverse sexual or gender identity can result in a lot of stress, anxiety, and even depression, so it's really important that we all support [*name of sex- or gender-diverse family member*].

We also know that with love and support, you are less likely to struggle emotionally and more likely to integrate this into your life beautifully. It's also really important to know that having a sexual or gender identity that is different from your family is not at all pathological, meaning that it is not a physical or mental disease, and that there is absolutely nothing wrong with you. And I want you to know that you have a right to be respected for who you are, how you identify, and what your pronouns are.

# Questions to Explore with Family Members

1. Can you each share how you are feeling in this moment?

_____

_____

2. How much time have you had to process this new knowledge?

_____

_____

3. Are you able to remember that, first and foremost, you are a family?

_____

_____

4. Do you feel confident that I am here to help you learn and support one another through this process?

_____

_____

5. (LGTBQ+ family member) How are you feeling right now?

_____

_____

6. (LGTBQ+ family member) How was your experience of sharing this with your family?

_____

_____

7. Is there anything that any of you need in order to feel comfortable working together and doing the home assignments?

_____

_____

I'm going to send you home today with one of two sex and gender identity assignments that are going to benefit you in three ways:

1. First, you are going to have an opportunity to share your feelings and questions, to develop new awareness about sex and gender diversity, and to connect as an accepting and loving family.

2. Next, you are going to learn that sexuality and gender identity is only one of the many aspects of identity.

3. Finally, you are going to read and commit to a family acceptance plan that communicates love, acceptance, and support for your loved one.

*Remember that you all are allowed to have the feelings you have.*
*Be kind and loving to one another.*

# Sexuality and Gender Identity
## Conversation

*When all Americans are treated as equal, no matter
who they are or whom they love, we are all more free.*
—Barack Obama

Create a comforting environment where you can have a loving conversation about sexuality and gender identity. Make sure that everyone is comfortable, turn your phones off, light a candle, and take a moment to close your eyes, take a few deep breaths, and then be present. You may choose a family member to take some notes or simply talk and listen.

1. Are we all able to agree that loving one another as a family has nothing to do with sexuality and gender identity?

_____

_____

_____

2. Are we all committed to learning more about sexuality and gender identity?

_____

_____

_____

3. (LGTBQ+ family member) How was your experience of sharing your sexuality or gender identity with us?

_____

_____

_____

4. (LGTBQ+ family member) What feelings are you having in general?

_____

_____

_____

5. (LGTBQ+ family member) How can we help you with other aspects of your life? Friends? School?

_____

_____

_____

6. What are some of your concerns about [*name of sex- or gender-diverse family member*]'s sexuality or gender identity?

_____

_____

_____

7. What do we understand about "minority stress" and the impact it might have on [*name of sex- or gender-diverse family member*]?

_____

_____

_____

8. How can we help to support [*name of sex- or gender-diverse family member*] with minority stress?

_____

_____

_____

9. (LGTBQ+ family member) Will you promise to let us know if you are experiencing any bullying or harassment so we can help you?

_____

_____

_____

10. Other than the gender we identify with, and whom we are attracted to, what defines us?

_____

_____

_____

# Our Family Acceptance Plan

Accepting, loving, and supporting an LGBTQ+ child and adolescent greatly reduces their risk of mental health disorders. It also helps them to feel pride in their identity and to integrate it into a life of meaning and purpose.

Take turns reading the following commitments to your loved one to reassure them of your love, support, and acceptance.

**I commit to...**

1. Recognizing and respecting your sexuality and gender identity as a normal, universal, and non-pathological part of your human experience.

2. Supporting your gender expression.

3. Using your chosen name and the pronoun that matches your gender identity.

4. Taking you to LGBTQ+ groups and events that you would like to attend.

5. Making sure that family members and all others treat you with respect.

6. Standing up for you when others mistreat you because of your LGBTQ+ identity.

7. Welcoming any of your LGBTQ+ friends.

8. Connecting you with LGBTQ+ adult role models.

9. Participating in family support groups and activities for families with LGBTQ+ children.

10. Reminding you every day how much I love you and value having you in my life.

Place this important family acceptance plan somewhere where you can see it each day, and remind yourselves what an amazing family you are.

# References

For your convenience, sample forms are available for download at www.pesi.com/familytherapy

## Part 1: Foundational Traits of Healthy Families

Baumrind, D. (2019). Parenting styles—characteristics and effects. Retrieved from *Parenting for Brain* (website). https://www.parentingforthebrain.com> 4-baumrind-parenting-styles

Beck, J. S. (1995). *Cognitive therapy: Basics and beyond.* New York: Guilford Press.

Carter, B., & McGoldrick, M. (1999). *The expanded family life cycle* (3rd ed.). Boston: Allyn & Bacon.

Gottman, J., & Silver, N. (1999). *The seven principles for making marriage work.* New York: Three Rivers Press.

Keirsey, D. (1998). *Please understand me II: Temperament, character, intelligence.* Del Mar, CA: Prometheus Nemesis Book Company.

McKay, M., & Fanning, P. (2000). *Self-esteem* (3rd ed.). Oakland, CA: New Harbinger Publications.

Ricker, A., Calmes, R. E., & Sneyd, L. W. (2006). *How happy families happen.* Center City, MN: Hazelden.

Yerkovick, M., & Yerkovich, K. (2011). *How we love our kids.* Colorado Springs, CO: Waterbrook Press.

## Part 2: Unique Family Challenges

Black, C. (1981). *Children of alcoholics: It will never happen to me.* New York: Random House.

Dattilio, F., & Jongsma, E. (2014). *The family therapy treatment planner.* Hoboken, NJ: John Wiley & Sons.

Doyle, R., & Nowinski, J. (2012). *Almost alcoholic: Is my (or my loved one's) drinking a problem?* Center City, MN: Hazelden

Evans, P. (2010). *The verbally abusive relationship* (3rd ed.). Avon, MA: Adams Media.

Hayes, S. C., & Smith, S. (2005). *Get out of your mind & into your life: The new acceptance & commitment therapy.* Oakland, CA: New Harbinger.

Johnson, S. (1996). *The practice of emotionally focused marital therapy: Creating connection.* Philadelphia: Bruner/Mazel.

Johnson, S. (2008). *Hold me tight.* New York: Little, Brown.

Kinoy, B. P. (2001). *Eating disorders: New directions in treatment and recovery.* New York: Columbia University Press.

Kübler-Ross, E., & Kessler, D. (2000). *Life lessons: Two experts on death and dying teach us about the mysteries of life and living.* New York: Scribner.

Lewis, J., Dana, R., & Blevins, G. (2002). *Substance abuse counseling* (3rd ed.). Pacific Grove, CA: Edith Beard Brady.

McKay, M., Fanning, P., & Paleg, K. (2006). *Couple skills: Making your relationship work* (2nd ed.). Oakland, CA: New Harbinger.

Meyer, I. H. (2003). Prejudice, social stress, and mental health in lesbian, gay, and bisexual populations: Conceptual issues and research evidence. *Psychological Bulletin, 129,* 674–697.

Nichols, M. (2020). *Gender expansive kids, polyamorous couples, and mostly heterosexual men: A therapist's guide to working with sex- and gender-diverse clients in the 21st century.* New York: Routledge Press.

Roszia, S., & Maxon, A. (2019). *Seven core issues in adoption and permanency: A comprehensive guide to promoting understanding and healing in adoption, foster care, kinship families, and third party reproduction.* Philadelphia: Jessica Kingsley.

Stroebe, M. (1993). *Handbook of bereavement: Theory, research, and intervention.* New York: Cambridge University Press.

Villapiano, M., & Goodman, L. (2001). *Eating disorders: Time for change.* Philadelphia: Brunner-Routledge.

Worden, J. W. (2018). *Grief counseling and grief therapy.* New York: Springer.